LETTERS FOR DIVORCE LAWYERS

Essential Communications for Clients, Opposing Counsel, and Others

MARTHA J. CHURCH

ABA General Practice, Solo & Small Firm Division

Cover design by ABA Publishing

10 09 08 07 06   5 4 3 2 1

Library of Congress Cataloging-in-Publication Data

Church, Martha J., 1942-
    Letters for divorce lawyers / Martha J. Church.
    p. cm.
    ISBN 1-59031-657-6
    1. Divorce suits—United States—Forms. 2. Lawyers—Records and correspondence—Forms. 3. Attorney and client—United States. 4. Legal correspondence—United States. 5. Form letters—United States. I. Title.

KF533.5.C48 2006
346.7301'660269—dc22   2006003917

Contents

CHAPTER 5

CHAPTER 6

CHAPTER 11

CHAPTER 15

CHAPTER 16

Acknowledgments

I would like to acknowledge Barry B. McGough, an excellent attorney, for demonstrating how family law should be practiced.

I would also like to acknowledge Mary Ann B. Oakley, an attorney who has been a friend since law school days, for her assistance and without whose help the production of this book would still be ongoing.

Finally, I would like to acknowledge Robert E. Andrews, deceased, an outstanding attorney who remained at all times the epitome of courtesy, civility and kindness, even in the most contentious matters.

Introduction

Why a book of letters for divorce lawyers? After all, we already have *Letters for Lawyers* and *Letters for Litigators*, both excellent books, so why another book of letters? Because, at least in part, divorce clients are a peculiar breed. I found it safest to assume that my divorce clients are acutely crazy. This is perfectly understandable. If a potential client is in your office getting information about a divorce or getting ready to file a divorce or needing to defend a divorce, that person's life has gone upside-down and you are on the front line with the wounded. To function successfully as a divorce attorney, you must have patience, compassion, and a strong self-protective instinct. In addition, to be truly successful, you need a large volume of new clients—there just is not that much repeat business in a divorce practice. In order to maintain your own sanity, you need systems, including an arsenal of letters.

In order to maintain your own sanity, you need systems, including an arsenal of letters.

According to Jill Wells Nunnally, a risk management attorney with Minnesota Lawyers Mutual, a legal malpractice carrier headquartered in Minneapolis, Minnesota, through calendar year 2005, 12.4 percent of all of its reported claims came from the family law area. MLM's data also indicates that 22.83 percent of all malpractice errors came from administrative mistakes and 21.88 percent came from client relations issues, for a total of 45 percent. Translated, this means that you could potentially affect 43 to 45 percent of your legal malpractice risk with better communications and administration/docket control.

To boil this down to the essentials, we have a high-volume business populated by crazy people who will sometimes take their feelings out on their lawyers. Consequently, lawyers who do divorce work need protection—and files filled with letters can provide at least some of this protection. This means real letters—not just e-mails and voicemails, helpful as those may be. Letters to the client do not always have to be *your* letters, either. You and your secretary should have an unbroken rule that a copy of *every single letter* in a case goes to the client, even if it is just a transmittal letter to the court clerk. Letters from you to opposing counsel, to the court, to experts, to whomever, will show the client CC'd at the bottom.

For letters you receive from opposing counsel, the court, the experts, whomever, invest in several rubber stamps. When the letter comes in, whoever opens it should date-stamp it with a stamp that includes either your name or your firm's name and the date. When you read the letter, you should stamp it with a stamp that says "Copy for your files." You add the date and your initials below the stamped image. Then, just before your secretary copies the letter, he also initials it. The client's copy now shows two stamps and the double set of initials, and you now have fairly conclusive evidence in your file that you mailed the copy. Not only does this look very official and remind the client that you are working on his or her case, you also have documentation that the client was informed of whatever—that the hearing was scheduled for a time certain or that the expert has accepted the engagement and what the fees will be. An example is included on page xvii. Some lawyers provide new clients with notebooks tabbed for pleadings and letters, along with a three-hole punch. This allows the client to feel organized and helps ensure that legal paperwork will be kept in one place—even if it is not always read.

This is all well and good, but who has time for all of this? That is where this book comes in. You know you need to send letters, but by the time you get back from court, go through your mail, answer phone calls, and attend to raging fires, you are brain-dead and do not have the creative energies to put together what you need. Go to this book, skim down the table of contents, find the subject you need—say, a letter to opposing counsel about overdue discovery responses (mild reminder)—and ask your secretary to rough this out for you in the Jones case. She takes the disk that came with this book, finds the letter, customizes it for your signature and the task is done, or at least a draft is ready for your tweaking. Or, you can always do the letter yourself if it is already 9:00 P.M., you want the letter faxed and mailed in the morning, and you have no life anyway.

This book is set up chronologically following the usual life of a case. I have tried to cover the most likely events in a typical divorce matter where a letter is suggested or demanded. I hope these letters will make your life easier and your malpractice insurance provider more content.

Finally, not all situations are covered in this book, and I refer you to two excellent books, *Letters for Litigators* and *The Complete Guide to Divorce Practice,* for additional examples of letters you might use.

Caveats

First, this book was written by a Georgia lawyer and occasionally refers to Georgia law. Be sure to customize any letter for your state's peculiarities.

Second, many of the letters included in this book were taken from actual files, so it has been necessary to remove identifying indicia. This process has made some of the wording a bit awkward, particularly with the use of names. Feel free to put names in your letters where mine show "your client" or "opposing counsel."

Third, for the same reason, all dates have been changed, mostly to 2005 and 2006. If the dates don't quite make sense, just pay attention to the overall content.

Fourth, I usually capitalize legal pleadings terms, especially when writing to clients. This helps the client differentiate the legalese and pick out the more important parts.

Finally, there are a few samples of advocacy letters and a couple of agreements. You will not be able to use these verbatim, but you might get some ideas for when you find yourself in similar situations.

Martha J. Church
mchurch@levinesmithlaw.com
(404) 237-5700

SUPERIOR COURTS

July 6, 1998

Ms. Martha J. Kuckleburg
One Atlantic Center
120 1 West Peachtree Street, N. E.
Suite 2000
Atlanta, GA 30309-3400

Dear Ms. Kuckleburg:

RE:

With reference to your July 2nd letter, I wish to advise as follows:

1. I will listen to the evidence at trial and make a decision as to the custody issue prior to the time the jury delebrates. The jury will then be asked to set child support based on the financial status of the non-custodial parent.

2. As soon as you file your motion to compel, we will set a hearing on this motion at the earliest possible time.

3. Ms. _____ in my office is in the process of attempting to reschedule the trial at a time other than during your requested leave of absence.

Sincerely yours,

Chief Judge

RBS/gcj
c:

COPY FOR YOUR FILE
HOLLAND & KNIGHT
7-7-98

RECEIVED
JUL 7 1998
MARTHA J. KUCKLEBURG

About the Author

Martha Kuckleburg Church is an attorney with Levine and Smith, an Atlanta, Georgia, law firm that specializes in family law. Ms. Church has represented clients in divorce and post-divorce matters for more than 25 years.

She received her B.A., cum laude, from Oglethorpe University and her J.D. and L.L.M. in taxation from the Emory Univerity School of Law. She has been active in and held leadership positions in the Family Law Sections of the Atlanta Bar Association and the State Bar of Georgia. She is also a member of the General Practice, Solo and Small Firm Section of the American Bar Association, where she serves as a member of the editorial board of *GPSolo*, the section magazine.

Initial Client Contact

As a divorce lawyer, you will frequently get calls from potential clients who got your name from someone at a cocktail party, from the family doctor, from the person you just met at the Chamber of Commerce meeting, or from your ad in the yellow pages. Some calls are cursory—they just want to know what your fees are or what your voice sounds like. Most callers will want to set up an appointment to meet with you—and some will want to tell you their life stories right then and there. Do you need a letter here? Possibly. If you got sucked into a lengthy conversation but the conversation was inconclusive (i.e., no appointment was made), then send a letter if you managed to get the caller's address. If an appointment was made, then send a letter to confirm the appointment. After the appointment, send a letter whether you were retained or not. And, of course, always send a letter to thank the person who made the referral to you.

Letter to Prospective Client When No Appointment Is Made but Prospect Has Been Served with a Complaint

Prospect Name
Address

Dear (Prospective Client):

It was good talking with you earlier today by telephone about your current situation. I know you have a lot to think about at this time. Although we discussed your pending divorce in some detail, I do want to point out that I am not representing you at this point. If you would like to proceed and have me represent you in this matter, please contact my office and set an appointment at your earliest convenience. Regardless, please bear in mind that you must file a written Answer with the Court within 30 days of the day you were served with the Divorce Complaint if you wish to fully protect yourself.

If I can be of additional assistance, please do not hesitate to let me know. I wish you the best with this matter.

Sincerely,

Attorney

Prospect Name
Address

Dear (Prospective Client):

This letter is to confirm your appointment with me for Monday, June 1, 2006, to discuss the Divorce Complaint your spouse has filed. Between now and our appointment, please make notes of questions as they occur to you, and bring your notes and the Complaint with you. If there are changes before our appointment, please do not hesitate to call.

Sincerely,

Attorney

CHAPTER

1

LETTERS FOR
DIVORCE
LAWYERS

Letter to Referral Source

Referral Source
Address

Dear (Referral):

    (Prospect or new client) has been in touch with me to review her current situation. I really appreciate the confidence you have shown in me by providing my name to her. Thank you.

                        Sincerely,

                        Attorney

Declination Letters

You have met with the prospect and spent an hour or two going over the situation—but the deal does not close. The person leaves, saying he wants to think about it; wants to talk with some other attorneys before making up his mind; or is just considering his options. Send a letter. Say you enjoyed meeting with him, you wish him the best, and you are *not* representing him. Make it clear that no attorney/client relationship was formed from that meeting. If there are any deadlines for him that you are aware of, like filing an Answer, for instance, remind him of that in your letter and urge him to protect himself. If it is your custom to charge for the initial consultation even if you are not hired, then it is especially important for you to send the letter reminding the prospect that the money paid was for the time already spent—and that you are not on retainer to do anything further.

Letter After Appointment When You Have Not Been Retained

Prospective Client
Address

Dear (Prospective Client):

The purpose of this letter is to review and summarize the conference you and I had in my office yesterday. During the conference you told me that you have decided to seek a divorce from your spouse. You told me that you have two children and that you are considering asking for joint custody of them. You also outlined your financial circumstances. I then gave you an outline of the divorce process and told you in general terms what you might expect. We also discussed the matter of attorney fees and, before you left, you paid my firm $_____.

After our conversation, you told me that you wanted to think more about the situation before going further, which I fully understand.

Although we discussed your divorce in some detail, I do want to point out and make sure you understand that you have not retained me to represent you. As I explained during our meeting, the fee you paid yesterday was for our time together and the information and advice I gave you then, and should not be construed as a retainer for any future services.

If you do decide that you would like me to represent you, please contact my office and make an appointment at your earliest convenience.

Sincerely,

Attorney

Letter After Appointment When You Have Not Been Retained and an Action Is Pending

Prospective Client
Address

Dear (Prospective Client):

The purpose of this letter is to review and summarize the conference you and I had in my office yesterday. During the conference you told me that your spouse has filed divorce proceedings in _____ Superior Court and that you were served with a copy yesterday. You told me that you do not want a divorce and that you wish to contest this action. You told me that you have two children and that you are considering asking for joint custody of them. You also outlined your financial circumstances. I then gave you an outline of the divorce process and told you in general terms what you might expect. We also discussed the matter of attorney fees.

After our conversation, you told me that you wanted to think more about the situation before going further, which I fully understand. Before you left, you paid my firm $ _____.

Although we discussed your divorce in some detail, I want to point out that you have not retained me to represent you. The fee you paid yesterday was for our time together and the information and advice I gave you then, and should not be construed as a retainer for future services. If you would like me to represent you, please contact my office and make an appointment at your earliest convenience.

Whatever you choose to do, please be advised that you have thirty (30) days from the date when you were served with the Divorce Complaint to file your written Answer with the Court if you want to fully protect yourself.

Please let me know if you have any questions. I wish you the best.

Sincerely,

Attorney

Retention Letters and Employment Contracts

You have met with the prospective client who has decided to retain you. What now? You need to immediately send this person a retention letter and/or an employment contract that spells out your agreement with that person: what you have been hired to do; what you have not been hired to do; what is included within the scope of your duties; what help you might need; who pays for that help; what this is going to cost; how it is going to be paid; when is it going to be paid; who is primarily responsible for paying it; and what happens if it is not paid. You *must* have a retention letter or an employment contract signed by both you and the client.

Client
Address

> Re: Plaintiff v. Defendant
> Superior Court of ____ County
> CAFN 12345A

Dear (Client):

Enclosed you will find two copies of a contract of employment for your representation in the post-divorce alimony modification matter filed by your former spouse. Please review the contract carefully and let me know if you have any questions. If not, please sign both copies and return them to me, along with your check for the retainer of $1,000. I will them sign them and return one to you for your files.

I look forward to hearing from you.

> Sincerely,

> Attorney

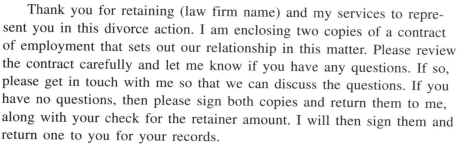

Client
Address

    Re: Plaintiff v. Defendant
        Superior Court of _____ County
        CAFN 12345A

Dear (Client):

    Thank you for retaining (law firm name) and my services to represent you in this divorce action. I am enclosing two copies of a contract of employment that sets out our relationship in this matter. Please review the contract carefully and let me know if you have any questions. If so, please get in touch with me so that we can discuss the questions. If you have no questions, then please sign both copies and return them to me, along with your check for the retainer amount. I will then sign them and return one to you for your records.

    Also enclosed is an Acknowledgment of Service. If you will date and sign this, have your signature notarized and return it to me, I will forward it to your spouse's attorney, (name).

    I look forward to talking with you next week so that we can begin moving your case forward toward a satisfactory resolution.

                Sincerely,

                Attorney

Client
Address

Re: Plaintiff v. Defendant
Superior Court of ＿＿＿ County
CAFN 12345A

Dear (Client):

I have prepared a Contract of Employment between you and me and my firm, two copies of which are enclosed. As we discussed, I will be billing for my services at the rate of $195.00 per hour. The contract reflects the retainer of $2,500.00 that you have paid and that will be held in my firm's trust account to be applied to the final bill according to the contract terms.

Please review the enclosed contract carefully and let me know if you have any questions. If the contract is acceptable, please sign both copies and return them to me. I will then sign them and return one to you for your files.

Sincerely,

Attorney

Transmittal Letter to Client With Signed Contract

CHAPTER

3

Retention Letters
and Employment
Contracts

Client
Address

    Re: Plaintiff v. Defendant
        Superior Court of _____ County
        CAFN 12345A

Dear (Client):

    Enclosed is one of the Contracts of Employment, which I have now signed. Please keep this with your important papers.

    I have mailed a Notice of Appearance to the Court Clerk, a copy of which is enclosed for your records. Within the next few days, I will prepare an Answer for filing and will send it to you first for your review. In the meantime, if you have any questions, please let me know.

                      Sincerely,

                      Attorney

CONTRACT OF EMPLOYMENT

_____, (hereinafter "Client" or "you") hereby employs (lead attorney name) and (firm name) (hereinafter "Attorneys" or "we") to represent Client in a domestic relations divorce action against (opposing party) and for such other related relief as may be required.

We accept this employment and agree to use our best efforts to represent you upon the following conditions:

(1) Legal services to be performed by us, and for which you are obligated to pay according to the terms of this Contract, include all of those actions which, in our judgment, are necessary for your adequate representation. Such actions may include, without limitation, preparing and filing pleadings, engaging in discovery, interviewing witnesses, reviewing and collating documentary and financial information, preparing for and participating in evidentiary proceedings, arguing motions, doing legal research, preparing legal memoranda and briefs, conferring with you, opposing counsel, or other persons (whether by telephone or personally), negotiating and drafting settlement contracts, preparing correspondence, and employing experts.

(2) You will immediately pay to us the sum of three thousand dollars ($3,000.00) as a deposit against legal fees to be earned and expenses that may be incurred by us on your behalf. Fees will be charged against the deposit at the hourly rates specified below.

You understand that we may periodically require the payment of additional deposits in such amounts as we may deem necessary to perform services required in your representation. You agree to pay any such deposits promptly and understand that failure to make such payments authorizes us to withdraw as counsel for you in any legal proceeding and to terminate our representation of you.

(3) You agree to pay us for your representation at the following rates:

Legal Assistant Time.....................$60.00 per hour
Associate Attorney Time................$100 to $135.00 per hour
Shareholder Attorney Time............ $165.00 to $240.00 per hour
Services performed by (lead attorney) shall be billed at the rate of $240.00 per hour.

(4) You also agree to pay any and all expenses incurred by us or our representatives on your behalf as the same accrue, including, but not limited to, court costs, official fees, costs for depositions, investigations, travel, copying, mileage, facsimile transmission, and long distance telephone charges.

(5) In the event we are still representing you on this matter one year from the date of this Contract, we reserve the right to change the billing rates to those rates that we are then charging new clients for similar representation.

(6) We agree to maintain complete and accurate records of time spent in your representation and to send you regular periodic billings describing the services rendered by us on your behalf during the period following the last such billing and showing the amounts earned as fees.

(7) We shall bill you approximately once a month. You agree to pay all sums due and owing for legal fees and expenses within ten (10) days of your receipt of each statement for services rendered.

(8) Should you fail to understand any aspect of your bill, it will be your responsibility to call us to have the matter clarified and explained. After one month has passed from your receipt of a monthly billing statement, it will be understood by us that you have accepted the accuracy of the billing statement as mailed.

(9) In the event you fail or refuse to pay any amounts due and owing, and fail to make payment arrangements satisfactory to us within ten (10) days of your receipt of any bill for services or expenses, then you consent to our withdrawal as your counsel upon notice as provided in Georgia Uniform Superior Court Rule 4.3. Furthermore, in the event it is necessary for us to pursue legal means to obtain payment for professional services or expenses, you agree to pay all amounts owed, plus fifteen percent (15%) and attorney fees, and all costs of collection.

(10) In the event you maintain a balance with us which is more than thirty (30) days past due, we shall have the right to charge interest on that past-due balance at the rate of one and one-half percent (1.5%) per month or eighteen percent (18%) per annum until the balance is paid.

(11) If the court should make an award to you of attorneys' fees and expenses of litigation to be paid by the adverse party, then that award, when actually paid to us, will be applied to the total fees earned by us in your representation plus the expenses incurred by us on your behalf. If the total of the award and/or amounts already paid by you to us exceeds the total of the fees and expenses charged by us, then you will be entitled to a refund of the excess.

CHAPTER

3

LETTERS FOR
DIVORCE
LAWYERS

If the total of the award and/or the amounts already paid by you to us is less than the total of the fees plus expenses charged by us, you are responsible for payment of the deficiency.

(12) You understand that we have neither represented nor guaranteed that the fees to be earned by us in representing you are limited in amount, except as to the hourly rates set forth in this Contract. You understand that the fee deposit paid to us pursuant to this Contract does not represent a minimum or maximum fee, nor does it represent a fixed portion of the total fee to be earned. You understand that the total fees to be earned pursuant to this Contract will be calculated by multiplying the total number of hours spent by us in providing services on your behalf by the appropriate billing rates set forth in paragraph (3).

(13) You acknowledge that we have made no guarantees regarding the successful outcome or termination of your representation, and all expressions relative thereto are matters of our <u>opinion</u> only.

This _____ day of _____, 2006.

CLIENT

_____

ATTORNEYS

_____

CONTRACT OF EMPLOYMENT

_____ (hereinafter "Client" or "you") hereby employs (lead attorney name) and (firm name) (hereinafter "Attorneys" or "we") to represent you in a domestic relations divorce action against (opposing party) under the following terms and conditions:

This representation is undertaken based upon your representations to us that you and your spouse have agreed on the primary matters that must be resolved during the divorce process, including but not limited to custody, visitation, child support, alimony, division of property, and payment of debts.

(1) Legal services to be performed by us, and for which you are paying according to the terms of this Contract, include and are limited to the following: conferring with you and opposing counsel, negotiating the fine points of your contract, drafting the Settlement Agreement, preparing correspondence, preparing and filing basic pleadings, and attending court with you at the final divorce hearing. We will NOT engage in discovery, interview witnesses, review or collate documentary and financial information, prepare for or participate in evidentiary proceedings, argue motions, do legal research or prepare legal memoranda or briefs, or employ experts.

(2) For the limited services described above, you will pay to us the sum of three thousand dollars ($3,000.00) as legal fees. One-half of this amount shall be paid now and is non-refundable. The remainder shall be paid at the time the Settlement Contract is signed.

(3) You understand that this Contract is based upon the assumption and your representations to us that your divorce case will remain uncontested through to the final hearing. Please be aware that if this case becomes contested, then this Contract shall be VOID and must be renegotiated or terminated. The determination that your case has become contested will occur at the time either party requests any assistance from the Court, either for discovery or for temporary or permanent relief. If the matter becomes contested, this event authorizes us to withdraw from this matter as counsel for you in any legal proceeding and to terminate our representation of you unless we and you have agreed on new terms.

(4) You acknowledge that we have made no guarantees regarding successful outcome or termination of your representation, and all expressions relative thereto are matters of our <u>opinion</u> only.

This _____ day of _____, 2006.

CLIENT

_____

ATTORNEYS

_____

Billing Letters

Sometimes it is necessary to communicate with your client about money—yours. Even though this topic should have been covered at length in your Retention Agreement, things change. You may need to send a collection letter, you may need to change the billing/payment terms, or you may need to set up an "evergreen" arrangement. Be sure to do this in writing and have your client confirm the communication and any new fee arrangement in writing.

Letter to Client—To Set Up Payment Plan

Client
Address

    Re: Plaintiff v. Defendant
       Superior Court of ____ County
       CAFN 12345A

Dear (Client):

As you are no doubt aware, you now have a significant past due balance of $5,000 on your account, even though our original Agreement calls for any outstanding balance to be paid in full each month. It is my preference that this amount be paid immediately. However, if you are not in a position to do this, then I propose that you pay the past due amount at the rate of $1,000 per month for five months. This payment, of course, will be in addition to the payment due each month for current services as we go forward.

If this is acceptable to you, please sign the enclosed copy of this letter and return it to me in the enclosed stamped envelope along with your check. If you have any questions or comments, please do not hesitate to let me know.

               Sincerely,

               Attorney

Client
Address

Re: Plaintiff v. Defendant
    Superior Court of ＿＿＿ County
    CAFN 12345A

Dear (Client):

You have a balance with my firm that is now more than 120 days past due. Please contact me immediately about your plans to pay this balance. If I do not hear from you within ten days of the date of this letter, I will have no choice but to turn this matter over for collection.

I look forward to speaking with you at your earliest opportunity.

Sincerely,

Attorney

Client
Address

Re: Plaintiff v. Defendant
    Superior Court of _____ County
    CAFN 12345A

Dear (Client):

Although our original fee agreement calls for you to pay your balance in full each month, you now have a significant past due balance of $5,000 on your account. Moreover, this is not the first time your account has been in arrears. In order for my firm to continue to represent you, we will have to modify our financial arrangement as follows. I require a payment from you of $10,000 immediately; $5,000 of that amount will be used to pay your past due balance, and the other $5,000 will be held against your final bill. In the meantime, you will be expected to pay each monthly invoice as it becomes due. If you do not timely pay a monthly invoice, we will then have no choice but (a) to use the funds we have been holding to pay that invoice, and (b) to withdraw from representing you in this case.

If these financial arrangements are acceptable to you, please sign the enclosed copy of this letter and return it to me in the enclosed stamped envelope along with your check for $10,000. Of course, if you have any questions or comments, please do not hesitate to let me know.

Sincerely,

Attorney

Client
Address

    Re: Plaintiff v. Defendant
       Superior Court of ____ County
       CAFN 12345A

Dear (Client):

    I have reviewed your billing file and find that we have not used any of your retainer amount to pay for a copy of the real estate appraisal. That being so, I suggest that we do nothing further about obtaining a copy of the written appraisal. The results, as we heard them, were not particularly helpful, so there is no benefit to having a written report.

    Also, we talked several weeks ago about the fact that it is necessary for you to make some payment on your account each month. So far, I have not received a payment since our conversation. Please make a payment on your account immediately.

    Let me know if you have any questions.

                    Sincerely,

                    Attorney

Client
Address

Re: Plaintiff v. Defendant
Superior Court of _____ County
CAFN 12345A

Dear (Client):

As you know from my voicemail message, I received your letter of instruction telling me that you had decided to drop your visitation modification case. Unfortunately, I had already done a good bit of research and had prepared a rough draft of a petition to modify visitation before I received your letter. I am enclosing copies of the Georgia Code and some Georgia cases that deal with these issues, which I found during my research.

Be that as it may, I hope things are going well for you. Please let me know if you have any questions or if I can be do anything further. I will send you an accounting and a refund of the unused portion of your retainer at the end of this billing cycle.

Very truly yours,

Attorney

Letter to Client About Closed Checking Account

Client
Address

    Re: Plaintiff v. Defendant
       Superior Court of _____ County
       CAFN 12345A

Dear (Client):

I have left a number of phone messages for you concerning your outstanding balance with my firm for $2,100. I am still holding your check for $1,500, which you gave me earlier for services before you closed the account. I do not wish to take further action to collect this money, but I feel that you have not acted in good faith with me, and I would like you to pay the outstanding balance immediately. At that time I will return your check.

If you have any questions, please let me know.

                Very truly yours,

                Attorney

Parent
Address

Re: Plaintiff v. Defendant
    Superior Court of _____ County
    CAFN 12345A

Dear (Parent):

At your request, I have checked with our bookkeeper on your daughter's account and have enclosed a summary for your review. The total fees charged are $5,966.53, and the total payments received to date are $4,147.40. This leaves an outstanding balance of $1,819.53 that is now due.

I hope this clears up any confusion, but if you do have additional questions or comments, please do not hesitate to give me a call.

Very truly yours,

Attorney

Letter to Client Who Has Questioned Fees

Client
Address

Re: Plaintiff v. Defendant
    Superior Court of _____ County
    CAFN 12345A

Dear (Client):

I have just received a notice that your case is number 99 on the Judge's trial calendar for the week of June 1. We are both required to be at the calendar call that morning at 9:30 A.M. in Courtroom Z. Other than this calendar notice, I have heard nothing from the Judge about our pending Motion. I continue to maintain that no news is good news.

Thank you for your letter of May 1, 2006, and your check for $2,000. I have reviewed your file and agree that your fees, to date, have been higher than I originally predicted. When I made that prediction, I took into account the fact that we would take depositions and have a temporary hearing; I did not know or take into account the fact that it would be necessary to have two hearings at the temporary hearing stage or that your former husband would have so many documents. I do keep careful records and have actually written off some charges from your account before you were billed. However, you are correct; $4,000 is a lot of money. I am glad you will be able to bring your account current this month, as you stated in your letter.

It does appear that, through our efforts, we have been able to defer any temporary modification for several months from the date of the original hearing, which should at least compensate somewhat for the higher fees. Given the fact that we are number 99 on the upcoming trial calendar, it does not appear that we will be actually reached for trial any time soon, particularly since we have filed a jury demand. In addition, when we finally do go to trial, much of what we prepared for the temporary hearings will be very useful, once updated.

I hope this information is useful to you and I welcome any comments you may have. Let me know if you have any questions; otherwise, I look forward to seeing you on June 1, 2006, at the Courthouse.

Very truly yours,

Attorney

Client
Address

    Re: Plaintiff v. Defendant
        Superior Court of _____ County
        CAFN 12345A

Dear (Client):

    Enclosed is a copy of the statement I have received from Professional Document Services in the amount of $189.65 for making copies of the documents provided by your spouse. Please pay this expense directly.

            Sincerely,

            Attorney

Letter to Client Requesting Additional Money for Expenses

Client
Address

Re: Plaintiff v. Defendant
Superior Court of _____ County
CAFN 12345A

Dear (Client):

I have met with the accountant, _____, who believes that he can give an estimate of the value of the business by looking at the sale of the _____ store. As you can see from the enclosed letter, he will not bill more than $2,000.00 without our prior agreement. I have used funds from your retainer account to pay $1,000.00. It is now necessary for you to replenish the retainer fund. I will need additional money for the accountant, as well as money for future depositions. After you have reviewed this letter, please give me a call and we will discuss our situation.

I look forward to hearing from you.

Sincerely,

Attorney

Withdrawal

Sometimes, despite your best efforts or perhaps in answer to your prayers, you have to withdraw from a case. This can be tricky depending on your jurisdiction, since you may need court approval in order to vacate the matter. Be certain that you document every step with correspondence, even if you have already had the conversation with the client. At a minimum, you will need a letter to the client, to the Court, and to opposing counsel.

Letter to Client that Attorney Is Withdrawing from Representation

Client
Address

Re: Plaintiff v. Defendant
Superior Court of ____ County
CAFN 12345A

Dear (Client):

As we discussed, it has become necessary for my firm to withdraw from you representation in this matter. (We have filed the Petition to Withdraw with the Court and the Judge has signed an order permitting us to withdraw effective immediately.)

It is my understanding that you have retained (new attorney) to represent you going forward. We will transfer your file to him immediately so that you and he will have time to prepare for the next hearing.

OR

It is my understanding that you have not retained an attorney to represent you going forward. As soon as you do, please have your new counsel contact me so that I can make arrangements to turn over your file. Please keep in mind that there is a hearing scheduled for Thursday, June 1, 2006.

OR

It is my understanding that you have chosen not to retain counsel and plan to represent yourself. We will have your file ready for you to pick up by next Monday. Please call my secretary and let him know when to expect you. Also keep in mind that there is a hearing scheduled for Thursday, June 1, 2006.

I wish you the best.

Sincerely,

Attorney

Client
Address

    Re: Plaintiff v. Defendant
       Superior Court of _____ County
       CAFN 12345A

Dear (Client):

    Please deem this letter as formal confirmation of my withdrawal as your attorney of record in the above-referenced matter, which we verbally agreed to during our conference this afternoon. Effective the date of this letter, your file in my office will be administratively closed.

    As of this date, no complaint has been filed. However, counsel for your spouse (name, address and telephone number of spouse's attorney) indicated last Friday that she would be sending a copy of the Complaint for Divorce with an Acknowledgment of Service shortly, which you said you would sign in lieu of service by the sheriff. As I told you this afternoon, I have not received a formal copy of the Complaint. However, after you left my office, I did receive a facsimile transmission, a copy of which I enclose for your convenience. I will notify your spouse's attorney immediately that we no longer represent you and provide contact information for you.

    I regret that we are unable to further represent you in this matter; however, should your new attorney wish to talk to me, I will be pleased to do so. I wish you the best of success in the future.

                Sincerely,

                Attorney

Formal Letter from Attorney to Client Withdrawing from
Representation—Form Required in Georgia

Client
Address

Re: Plaintiff v. Defendant
    Superior Court of _____ County
    CAFN 12345A

Dear (Client):

    This Notice is written pursuant to Georgia Superior Court Uniform Rule 4.3 to confirm that I plan to withdraw from representing you in the Court in this matter. Pursuant to this Rule, I am informing you of the following items:

    a. The Court continues to have jurisdiction in this matter;

    b. You will have the responsibility of keeping the Court informed of where papers or other notices should be served, mailed, or delivered;

    c. You will have the obligation to prepare for any trial in this matter or hire other counsel to do so (although no trial is set in this matter at this time);

    d. If you do not meet these obligations and requirements, you may suffer adverse consequences;

    e. The dates of any scheduled proceedings, including trial, will not be affected by my withdrawal. At this time, nothing is scheduled in Court to my knowledge;

    f. I am mailing this to you at your last known address.

    Ten (10) days from the date on this notice, I will file the Notice and a Petition to Withdraw with the Court. You will receive another letter from me at that time. You will have an additional ten (10) days to file objections with the Court if you wish.

    Please call me if you have any questions.

Sincerely,

Attorney

Letter from Former Counsel to New Counsel

CHAPTER

5

Withdrawal

New attorney
Address

    Re: Plaintiff v. Defendant
       Superior Court of _____ County
       CAFN 12345A

Dear (New Attorney):

    (Client) has informed me that you will be representing her going forward. I have submitted a formal Petition to Withdraw to the Court in the above-referenced case and I am enclosing a copy of the Notice of Withdrawal. At this time, I am waiting for the signed and stamped court copy. I will forward it to (client) as soon as I receive it. I have already given her a complete copy of her file to date.
    Please let me know if you have any questions.

              Sincerely,

              Former Attorney

Transmittal Letter to Clerk with Substitution of Counsel Notice

Clerk of Court
Address

Re: Plaintiff v. Defendant
    Superior Court of _____ County
    CAFN 12345A

Dear Clerk:

Enclosed please find a Notice of Substitution of Counsel for the Plaintiff to be filed in the above-referenced matter. I have also enclosed an additional copy of this Notice, and I would appreciate it if someone in your office would stamp the copy "filed" with the date and then return it to my office in the enclosed stamped, addressed envelope. If you have any questions, please let me know.

Thank you for your assistance in this matter.

Sincerely,

Attorney

Opposing Counsel
Address

    Re: Plaintiff v. Defendant
       Superior Court of _____ County
       CAFN 12345A

Dear (Opposing Counsel):

    This letter is to advise you that I now represent (Client) in the above-referenced matter. Enclosed please find the Notice of Substitution of Counsel that has been sent for filing with the Clerk of the Court.
    As soon as I have had an opportunity to review my client's file, I will be in touch. In the meantime, if you have any questions, please let me know.

               Sincerely,

               Attorney

Letter from Opposing Counsel to Newly Unrepresented Opposing Party

Opposing Party
Address

    Re: Plaintiff v. Defendant
       Superior Court of _____ County
       CAFN 12345A

Dear (Opposing Party):

    It is my understanding that (former attorney) no longer represents you. If she does still represent you or if you have obtained new counsel, please give him or her this letter and ask that I be contacted.

    I am enclosing a copy of the Divorce Complaint that I have filed and faxed to your former attorney, together with an Acknowledgment of Service. I would appreciate it if you would sign this in front of a notary and return it to me in the enclosed envelope. If I have not received the signed Acknowledgment within fourteen (14) days, I will arrange for service on you by the sheriff.

    I look forward to hearing from you or your new counsel as soon as possible.

                   Sincerely,

                   Opposing Counsel

Letter Notifying Opposing Counsel of Withdrawal

Opposing Counsel
Address

    Re: Plaintiff v. Defendant
       Superior Court of _____ County
       CAFN 12345A

Dear (Opposing Counsel):

    This is to inform you that, effective immediately, this firm no longer represents (client) in the above-referenced matter. We have turned over her file and you should be receiving a Notice of Appearance from her new attorney shortly. (Client) and her new counsel are aware that there is a hearing scheduled for Thursday, June 1, 2006.
    Please let me know if you have any questions.

              Sincerely,

              Former Attorney

Letter to the Court Re: Withdrawal if No Petition Is Required

Judge
Address

    Re: Plaintiff v. Defendant
       Superior Court of _____ County
       CAFN 12345A

Dear (Judge):

This is to inform you that, effective immediately, this firm no longer represents (client) in the above-referenced matter. We have turned over her file to her, and her new attorney should be filing a Notice of Appearance shortly. (Client) and her new counsel are both aware that there is a hearing scheduled for Thursday, June 1, 2006.

Please let me know if you have any questions.

       Sincerely,

       Former Attorney

Discharged Counsel
Address

    Re: Plaintiff v. Defendant
       Superior Court of _____ County
       CAFN 12345A

Dear (Discharged Counsel):

    Enclosed is a duplicate of the Answer and Counterclaim in the above-referenced matter.

    As we discussed, you have agreed to forward the Answer to your former client. I am disappointed that she terminated your services. I enjoyed working with you and I look forward to doing so again.

    Thank you for your attention to this matter.

                    Very truly yours,

                    Opposing Counsel

5

Letter to Opposing Counsel from Replacement Counsel

Opposing Counsel
Address

    Re: Plaintiff v. Defendant
       Superior Court of _____ County
       CAFN 12345A

Dear (Opposing Counsel):

I will be working with (client) toward the successful completion of this matter. Enclosed please find a copy of my Notice of Appearance. I am also enclosing a proposed Settlement Agreement that has been approved by my client. Please discuss this with your client at your earliest convenience, and let me know if we might settle the case along these lines. I look forward to hearing from you.

          Sincerely,

          New Attorney

Discharged Counsel
Address

    Re: Plaintiff v. Defendant
       Superior Court of _____ County
       CAFN 12345A

Dear (Discharged Counsel):

    I have been retained to represent (Client) in the above-referenced case. I am enclosing a copy of my Notice of Appearance for your records. If you have submitted a formal withdrawal, I would be most appreciative if you would forward a copy to me, along with those parts of the file that you believe will be helpful. Thank you very much for your assistance in this matter.

                Sincerely,

                New Attorney

CHAPTER

5

LETTERS FOR
DIVORCE
LAWYERS

Client
Address

Re: Plaintiff v. Defendant
    Superior Court of _____ County
    CAFN 12345A

Dear (Client):

I will have the file transferred to your new attorney shortly, although I am hoping that you and your spouse will be able to work this out without considerable attorney involvement.

Very truly yours,

Former Attorney

Letter from Former Attorney to Replacement Re: File Transfer

CHAPTER

5

Withdrawal

New Attorney
Address

    Re: Plaintiff v. Defendant
        Superior Court of _____ County
        CAFN 12345A

Dear (New Attorney):

    I have received a copy of your Notice of Substitution of Counsel in the above-referenced case. I should have the file ready to be picked up by early next week. If you need anything sooner than that, please let me know.

            Very truly yours.

            Old Attorney

45

Transmittal Letter from Discharged Attorney to New Counsel with File

New Attorney
Address

Re: Plaintiff v. Defendant
Superior Court of _____ County
CAFN 12345A

Dear (New Attorney):

Attached is the file for (Client), including the following:

1. Three white binders, which contain documents produced by (client);

2. A black notebook, which includes all the pleadings to date;

3. A red weld with document copies from opposing counsel, which I reviewed but have not organized; and

4. Subpoenas that were served on opposing party's doctor and _____ Hospital for her records. Her attorney objected, and the matter has not been pushed. The Answer was filed July 19, so discovery will expire in January.

I believe I have included everything in this file that is relevant or might be helpful. If you have any questions or if I can be of additional assistance, please let me know.

Very truly yours,

Former Attorney

New Attorney
Address

    Re: Plaintiff v. Defendant
        Superior Court of _____ County
        CAFN 12345A

Dear (New Attorney):

    I have submitted a formal withdrawal in the above-referenced case, a copy of which is enclosed. At this time, I am waiting for the signed court copy. I will forward it to (Client) as soon as I receive it. I have also sent her a complete copy of her file to date.

                Sincerely,

                Discharged Attorney

Pleadings Transmittal Letters

Although pleadings are self-explanatory to those in the know, it is polite, as well as a good idea, to include a transmittal letter to the Court with a copy to your client when you file something. Of course, it is also an excellent idea to send a draft of any pleading to your client before filing, asking the client to review for additions, changes, and corrections before the document is finalized and served on the opposing counsel. If the pleading has to be verified, then, of course, you must have the client review it before signing the verification. If you are sending the client a copy of a Complaint or Answer you have received from opposing counsel, you also need to explain what it is and how to deal with it.

Clerk of Court
Address

Re: Plaintiff v. Defendant
    Superior Court of _____ County
    CAFN 12345A

Dear (Clerk):

Please find enclosed Defendant's Answer in the above-referenced case. Also enclosed are Defendant's Interrogatories, Request for Production of Documents, and Notice to Produce Documents. Please file the originals, stamp the copies and return them to me in the enclosed stamped envelope.

If you have any questions, please let me know. Thank you for your assistance in this matter.

Sincerely,

Attorney

Client
Address

   Re: Plaintiff v. Defendant
       Superior Court of ____ County
       CAFN 12345A

Dear (Client):

Enclosed you will find the following documents:

   1.   A draft of a Complaint for Divorce. Please review this carefully
for accuracy and let me know if we need to make any changes before
we file it and serve a copy on your spouse. Please also let me know if
you believe we will need a court hearing shortly. If so, I will revise this
to set out problem areas and ask for a temporary hearing. I will discuss
this with you further before we file.
   2.   An original Verification. With this document, you are swearing
that the facts set out in the Complaint are true and correct to the best of
your knowledge. Please date and sign this, have your signature notarized and return it to me. I will attach it to the final version of the Complaint for Divorce when it is filed.
   3.   Notice to Produce/Request for Production of Documents. These
will be served on your husband, asking that he produce documents so
that we can determine and verify the current assets and financial situation. Please review these and let me know if we need to add further
requests.
   4.   Interrogatories. This document includes a list of written questions that your husband must answer, under oath. Please let me know of
any additional questions you think we should ask.
   5.   Financial Affidavit Form. The purpose of this form is to set out
your financial situation to the best of your knowledge. It calls for you to
list assets, liabilities, income, and expenses. The Judge will rely on the
financial affidavit at a temporary hearing to decide the temporary use of
property and temporary support. Please start working on this at your
earliest opportunity because we will have to file it if, or when, we ask
for a temporary hearing.

After you have reviewed and digested all of this, please call me so that we can discuss the next steps.

Sincerely,

Attorney

Client
Address

   Re: Plaintiff v. Defendant
       Superior Court of _____ County
       CAFN 12345A

Dear (Client):

Enclosed are copies of documents I have just received from your spouse's attorney who is preparing to file the Divorce Complaint. Included you will find the following:

   1. <u>An Original Acknowledgment of Service</u>. Please date and sign this, have your signature notarized, and return the original to me. Keep the copy for your files. If we do not return this, the Sheriff will serve you with a copy of the Divorce Complaint.
   2. <u>The Divorce Complaint</u>. We will be filing an Answer in response to the Complaint shortly.
   3. <u>Plaintiff's First Interrogatories to Defendant</u>. These are written questions, which require sworn written answers from you and will be due within the next few weeks.
   4. <u>Plaintiff's First Request for Production of Documents to Defendant</u>. This contains the list of documents that your spouse's attorney wants to review. We will have to provide those documents that you have in your possession when we provide the written answers to the Interrogatories. It would be a good idea to begin gathering these documents together.

There is no temporary hearing scheduled yet, but if we are not able to work out matters on a temporary basis with your spouse, we will ask for one.

After you have reviewed the enclosures, please give me a call so that we can discuss our next steps.

                           Sincerely,

                           Attorney

53

Transmittal Letter to Client with Draft of Answer, Counterclaim
and Discovery Pleadings

Client
Address

      Re: Plaintiff v. Defendant
         Superior Court of _____ County
         CAFN 12345A

Dear (Client):

Enclosed you will find the following pleadings that we have prepared to be filed on your behalf after you review them:

1. A draft of our Answer to your spouse's Divorce Complaint. Please
compare the Answer, paragraph by paragraph, to the Complaint to make
sure that our Answer is accurate. Let me know if we need to make any
changes before it is filed.

2. A draft of our Counterclaim. In effect, this is your divorce complaint. It sets out the situation from your point of view. Please review
carefully for accuracy and completeness.

3. A Verification to the Answer and Counterclaim. With this document you are swearing that the facts set out in the Answer and Counterclaim are true to the best of your knowledge. Please date and sign this,
have your signature notarized and return it to me. I will attach it to the
Answer when it is filed.

3. A draft of Interrogatories. Your spouse is required to give written
answers, under oath, to these questions. Do we want to add any more?

4. A draft of a Notice to Produce/Request for Production of Documents. Do we want to ask for any additional documents?

5. A draft of a Financial Affidavit. We will need this for the temporary hearing now scheduled for June 1. I suggest you review your credit
card statements and your bank records for the last year in order to get
averages for the expenses in your budget. This document should be
reflective of your budget before the separation.

Finally, you should also begin gathering the documents that are listed in the Notice to Produce, which was served with the Complaint. We are required to make those available to your spouse's attorney for review and copying within a few weeks.

Please call me if you have questions. I look forward to talking with you.

Sincerely,

Attorney

Transmittal Letter to Client with Answer and Discovery from Opposing Counsel

Client
Address

Re: Plaintiff v. Defendant
    Superior Court of _____ County
    CAFN 12345A

Dear (Client):

Enclosed are several things I have just received from your spouse's attorney:

1. <u>An Answer and Counterclaim</u>. In order to make sense of the Answer, you must compare it, paragraph by paragraph, to our Complaint for Divorce. The Counterclaim is your spouse's version of a divorce complaint;

2. <u>Defendant's Request for Production of Documents and Notice to Produce to Plaintiff</u>. This is the list of documents that we are required to produce to your spouse's attorney within thirty (30) days. Of course, if you do not have the documents, then we cannot produce them. To the extent that you do have the documents, however, please start gathering them together so that we can get this organized soon;

3. <u>Defendant's First Continuing Interrogatories to Plaintiff</u>. There are sixteen (16) written questions in these Interrogatories to which we are required to give written, verified Responses within thirty (30) days. The first five questions are self-explanatory. I will take care of number 6. The remaining questions are also self-explanatory. After you have worked out rough drafts of your answers, we will review and refine them.

Please let me know if you have any questions.

Sincerely,

Attorney

Client
Address

    Re: Plaintiff v. Defendant
       Superior Court of _____ County
       CAFN 12345A

Dear (Client):

    Enclosed is a draft of an Answer and Counterclaim that we have prepared to file in your case. Please review this carefully and compare it, paragraph by paragraph, to your husband's Divorce Complaint. If we have made any errors, please let me know. Then please review the Counterclaim and let me know if we need to make any changes, additions, or corrections before we finalize it.

    Finally, enclosed is an original Verification. Please date and sign this, have your signature notarized, and return it to me. As soon as we receive the Verification and have your approval, we will file the Answer and Counterclaim.

    I look forward to hearing from you.

               Sincerely,

               Attorney

Letter to Unrepresented Defendant that Complaint Has Been Filed

Opposing Party
Address

Re: Plaintiff v Defendant
Superior Court of _____ County
CAFN 12345A

Dear (Opposing Party):

Your spouse, (client), has retained this firm to represent her in connection with a divorce and dissolution of your marriage. Toward that end, we will file a Complaint for Divorce in _____ Superior Court on June 1, 2006. I am enclosing the service copy of that Complaint, along with the other Family Court documents, which we are required by the Court to provide to you.

In addition, I am enclosing an original Acknowledgment of Service to avoid the necessity of having a Sheriff's deputy personally hand these documents to you. If you will be kind enough to date and sign the Acknowledgment, have your signature notarized, and return it to me in the envelope provided, I will be responsible for filing it with the Court. I will then provide you (or your attorney, if you are represented) with a copy marked "filed." If I do not receive the signed Acknowledgment from you within ten (10) days, I will make arrangements to have you personally served. Of course, if you have retained counsel, please take these documents to your attorney at your earliest opportunity.

Finally, I would appreciate hearing from you or your attorney, if you are represented, as quickly as possible so that we can begin to deal with the issues in an expeditious, professional, and amicable manner. It is my desire to resolve this case in that fashion, and it is my hope that you and your attorney feel similarly. If that is the case, then the chances of achieving that goal are increased dramatically.

Very truly yours,

Attorney

Financial Affidavit

This is probably the single most important document in the usual divorce case. To the client, it looks like Greek, especially if the client is mathematically challenged. The better practice is to bring the client in and do the Financial Affidavit together, but this is not always possible, so a letter to the client explaining the process is necessary. This is a good place to emphasize that the Financial Affidavit should be based on reality and not wishful thinking.

Transmittal Letter to Client with Financial Affidavit

Client
Address

Re: Plaintiff v. Defendant
    Superior Court of _____ County
    CAFN 12345A

Dear (Client):

Enclosed you will find a copy of the standard Financial Affidavit form that is used in divorce cases in the Superior Court of _____ County. Each party is required to prepare one to submit to the Court in any contested hearing. Your spouse is also required to complete this form.

You will note that there are three parts:

1. The first part is for basic information about you, your spouse, and the children and is mostly self-explanatory.

2. The second section is for listing all assets and liabilities. This section is broken into subcategories for assets, such as real property, retirement accounts, and automobiles, and liabilities, such as mortgages, car loans, and credit card debts.

3. The final section is for income and expenses. The income part is relatively simple, and most of it will come from your paycheck stub. The expense section is primarily your monthly budget. Consult your checkbook and credit and debit card statements for this information. I suggest you go through these records for at least 12 months. This way you can get averages for things like groceries and eating out, plus you will be reminded of periodic expenses such as semi-annual insurance premiums and back-to-school clothes for the children.

When you have roughed this in, we will get together and review it. In the meantime, if you have questions about how to handle any aspect of it, please do not hesitate to give me a call.

Sincerely,

Attorney

Client
Address

  Re: Plaintiff v. Defendant
      Superior Court of ____ County
      CAFN 12345A

Dear (Client):

  Enclosed is a copy of your spouse's Domestic Relations Financial Affidavit. I think you will be able to take some of the information from this to plug into your spreadsheet. I am also enclosing her Interrogatory Responses and Responses to the Request for Production for your review. If you have any of the required documents in your possession that she does not include, we need to get those together as well.

  As a reminder, you and I will meet at 1:00 P.M., on Thursday, June 1, 2006, to review documents and the spreadsheet. I have talked to your spouse's attorney and we have scheduled a joint meeting at her office for 10:00 A.M., on Friday, June 2, 2006, assuming that that time works with your and your spouse's schedule.

  Please let me know if you have any questions; otherwise, I will see you on June 1.

                    Sincerely,

                    Attorney

Written Discovery

F ew would argue that discovery is the guts of the case. You probably have your stock Notices to Produce/Request for Production and your Interrogatories. You can recite them in your sleep. However, your client does not have a clue what these are, and it is up to you to educate him or her about the process. While all divorce cases have basic similarities, each one has its own nuances, and you can only get those from your client. For that reason, it is helpful to have a letter of explanation to send along with a draft of your discovery requests so that your client can help you do the fine-tuning. Then, when your client is on the receiving end, it is good to have a letter of explanation and encouragement so that you can lessen the blow of the amount of work that will be required to comply fully and so that you can emphasize the necessity of full disclosure. In addition, there are also letters to the client to accompany discovery responses from the opposing party so you can encourage your client to review them and comment.

A second aspect of discovery is with opposing counsel and maybe the Court. The first phase is just the regular transmittal letter. Then there are the letters that deal with the tardy responses and the nonexistent responses. Court rules usually require attempts to resolve discovery disputes before Motions to Compel can be filed.

Transmittal Letter to Client with Discovery Filed by Opposing Counsel

Client
Address

    Re: Plaintiff v. Defendant
        Superior Court of _____ County
        CAFN 12345A

Dear (Client):

Enclosed you will find the following:

1. A copy of Defendant's Interrogatories to Plaintiff consisting of twenty-one (21) questions attached to the Introduction. These questions will require your written answers. Please start working on your answers by making notes for each question; and

2. Defendant's First Request for Production and Notice to Produce. Here, there are twenty-eight (28) listed types of documents requested. It may be that you have no documents responsive to some of these; however, you do need to begin gathering together those documents that you do have.

We have approximately three weeks to assemble these materials. Please let me know if you have any questions on the enclosures. Otherwise, I will be in touch with you shortly.

        Sincerely,

        Attorney

Client
Address

Re: Plaintiff v. Defendant
    Superior Court of _____ County
    CAFN 12345A

Dear (Client):

Your spouse's attorney, _____, has now filed formal discovery in this matter, copies of which are enclosed. Mr. _____ is entitled to responses by the third week in May. Should you receive this letter in time, please bring whatever documents you can find with you to our scheduled meeting next Monday afternoon. I look forward to hearing from you or seeing you next Monday.

Sincerely,

Attorney

Transmittal Letter to Client with Opposing Party's Discovery Responses

Client
Address

Re: Plaintiff v. Defendant
    Superior Court of _____ County
    CAFN 12345A

Dear (Client):

Enclosed you will find the following:

1. Your spouse's response to our Notice to Produce and Request for Production of Documents. This is not particularly helpful, but I have reviewed and inventoried the produced documents and she has given us a fair number;

2. Your spouse's responses to our written Interrogatories. These are fairly comprehensive but do not give much information about the business. There are two income and expense statements attached for 2004 and 2005; the summary page for 2005 is missing.

3. Plaintiff's First Interrogatories to Defendant served by your spouse's attorney. We will need to provide written responses to these by the third week of June. For now, only deal with those for which you have concrete answers.

4. Plaintiff's Notice to Produce and Requests for Production of Documents served by your spouse's attorney. You are required to provide these documents within thirty (30) days. Please gather together all the documents that you have. I realize that many of the records are in the possession of your spouse, so we will not worry about these now.

If you have any questions about this, please let me know. Otherwise, we can discuss these when we meet on June 1, 2006.

Very truly yours,

Attorney

Client
Address

Re: Plaintiff v. Defendant
    Superior Court of ____ County
    CAFN 12345A

Dear (Client):

Enclosed are several things I have just received from your spouse's attorney:

1. An Answer and Counterclaim. In order to make sense of the Answer, you must compare it, paragraph by paragraph, to our Complaint for Divorce. The Counterclaim is your spouse's version of a divorce complaint.

2. Defendant's Request for Production of Documents and Notice to Produce to Plaintiff. This is the list of documents that we are required to produce to your spouse's attorney within thirty (30) days. Of course, if you do not have the documents, then we cannot produce them. However, to the extent you do have the documents, please start gathering them together.

3. Defendant's First Continuing Interrogatories to Plaintiff. There are sixteen (16) written questions in these Interrogatories to which we are required to give written, verified Responses within thirty (30) days. The first five questions are self-explanatory. I will take care of number 6. The remaining questions are also self-explanatory. After you have worked out rough drafts of your answers, we will review and refine them.

Please let me know if you have any questions.

Sincerely,

Attorney

CHAPTER

8

LETTERS FOR
DIVORCE
LAWYERS

Transmittal Letter to Client with Responses from Opposing Party

Client
Address

Re: Plaintiff v. Defendant
 Superior Court of ____ County
 CAFN 12345A

Dear (Client):

Enclosed are Interrogatory Responses that we have received from your spouse; please ignore the first two pages and start with the answers on the third page. If you would review these, so that we might talk about them next Monday, that would be most helpful. I look forward to seeing you then.

Sincerely,

Attorney

Client
Address

Re: Plaintiff v. Defendant
Superior Court of _____ County
CAFN 12345A

Dear (Client):

Enclosed is the Response to our Request for Production of Documents, which we have received from your spouse. This is all we received; there were no documents. Please compare this Response, paragraph by paragraph, to our Notice to Produce/Request for Production of Documents. Then let me know if his answers, at least when he says that certain documents are in your possession, are accurate. In the meantime, if we get your husband's Interrogatory Responses, I will forward those to you as well.

Sincerely,

Attorney

Client
Address

Re: Plaintiff v. Defendant
   Superior Court of _____ County
   CAFN 12345A

Dear (Client):

   I reviewed most of your spouse's documents at her attorney's office yesterday. I also picked up her supplemented Interrogatory Responses and Document Responses, copies of which are enclosed. In looking through her answers, the thing that strikes me is that you would be well served to <u>immediately</u> discontinue any further personal conversations with her. I have a plaque on the wall in my office that says, "A Closed Mouth Gathers No Foot." Please keep this in mind.

   At your earliest opportunity, review her Responses, and let me know if you see anything seriously out of line.

   Also enclosed is a credit card bill that came to your house. I opened it at (opposing counsel)'s office so they could make copies. Please pay this directly.

                              Very truly yours,

                              Attorney

Opposing Counsel
Address

Re: Plaintiff v. Defendant
Superior Court of _____ County
CAFN 12345A

Dear (Opposing Counsel):

According to my records, your client was served with Interrogatories and a Request for Production of Documents with the original Complaint. His Acknowledgment is dated March 9, 2006, and it was filed March 13, 2006. Either way, I believe his responses are now due. I look forward to receiving them from him at your earliest opportunity.

Sincerely,

Attorney

Letter to Opposing Counsel Re: Incomplete Discovery Responses

Opposing Counsel
Address

> Re: Plaintiff v. Defendant
> Superior Court of _____ County
> CAFN 12345A

Dear (Opposing Counsel):

I have reviewed the documents produced by your client and find that many are missing. Pursuant to Superior Court Rule 6.4(B), please consider this my good faith effort to resolve this matter, short of filing a Motion to Compel, by asking that your client produce the documents listed in the attachment to this letter prior to the close of business June 1, 2006. If the documents are not produced by that time, I will have no choice but to file the Motion to Compel.

Thank you for your assistance in this matter.

Sincerely,

Attorney

Opposing Counsel
Address

    Re: Plaintiff v. Defendant
        Superior Court of _____ County
        CAFN 12345A

Dear (Opposing Counsel):

After a thorough review of the documents provided to me from your client, I find I am missing the following:

1. Pay stubs from November 15, 2005, until January 10, 2006;
2. W-2 for 2005;
3. Statements from her retirement accounts;
4. All bank statements, cancelled checks, etc., after August 6, 2005 and prior to July 7, 2004. I also need all bank registers for that period of time; and
5. The current Financial Affidavit.

Please forward these documents to me at your earliest opportunity

        Sincerely,

        Attorney

Detailed Letter to Opposing Counsel Re: Missing Discovery

Opposing Counsel
Address

Re: Plaintiff v Defendant
    Superior Court of _____ County
    CAFN 12345A

Dear (Opposing Counsel):

It has been almost two months since we were last in Court, at which time you promised to send me your client's documents. To date, I have received nothing. So that this will be clearly understood, I am going to refer to my Request for Production of Documents, number by number.

1. No problem.
2. Is she reimbursed by her employer for any reason? If so, we have no Response or documents.
3. The 2005 income tax return, which is due April 15th, would be responsive to this number.
4. No problem.
5. We have received four or five paycheck stubs and a 2003 W-2. Please provide the remaining paycheck stubs from the time she began working again in September 2004 through her most recent paycheck stub, which should be for March 31, 2005.
6. The only bank record we have received is one monthly statement for _____ Bank Account No. _____; the August 6, 2005 statement.
8. We need credit card statements before and after the July 22 statement for the MasterCard, as well as statements for other credit card accounts.
23. No problem.
24. Again, we need information on her retirement accounts.
25. Does she have any installment obligations? If so, we have no documents for No. 25.
26. No problem.
27. We need an up-to-date resume.
28. No problem.

Please consider this to be my good faith effort to resolve these matters as required by Uniform Superior Court Rule 6.4(B). If I have had no response from you by June 15, 2006, 1 will proceed with a Motion to Compel.

Sincerely,

Attorney

Perseverance—Another Letter to Opposing Counsel
Re: Missing Discovery

Opposing Counsel
Address

Re: Plaintiff v. Defendant
Superior Court of _____ County
CAFN 12345A

Dear (Opposing Counsel):

I have received your latest packet of documents but find that we are still short a number of things. Those missing documents are specified on the attached list. Please have your client produce these immediately so that I do not have to go forward with the Motion to Compel. Thank you for your assistance in this matter.

Also, enclosed are copies of my client's updated documents pursuant to your request to supplement.

Sincerely,

Attorney

Opposing Counsel
Address

Re: Plaintiff v. Defendant
    Superior Court of ____ County
    CAFN 12345A

Dear (Opposing Counsel):

As you are well aware, your client has failed or refused to produce many of the documents that I have requested in this case. We must move forward with discovery and expert depositions, and I am unable to prepare for those depositions without your client's documents.

I really do not want to file a Motion to Compel, but I believe that I have extended every courtesy and I am at the limit of my patience. In the best interest of my client, I have enclosed a copy of the Motion that I intend to file by 10:00 A.M. on Friday, May 12, 2006, if the documents are not produced or made available for my inspection prior to that date.

For your convenience, I have enclosed a list of specific documents that I expect to receive from your client.

Sincerely,

Attorney

Opposing Counsel
Address

Re: Plaintiff v. Defendant
    Superior Court of ____ County
    CAFN 12345A

Dear (Opposing Counsel):

Enclosed please find my client's response to your Motion to Compel Discovery, which I filed on July 11, 2006. As part of the response to your Motion to Compel, I am supplementing my earlier responses with copies of additional documents that, hopefully, will satisfy your apparent never-ending need for more paper. The additional documents I am providing contemporaneously with this response number 674 pages. Please review my response carefully, and, hopefully, the confusion that has been created by the production of the earlier documents will be eliminated.

If I can be of further assistance to you, please do not hesitate to call me.

Sincerely,

Attorney

Opposing Counsel
Address

Re: Plaintiff v. Defendant
    Superior Court of _____ County
    CAFN 12345A

Dear (Opposing Counsel):

As you requested in your letter of June 1, 2006, my client has made the additional documents that he has in his possession, custody, or control available at our offices for your review. You may review these documents after you have returned the first set of original documents that were sent to you over a month ago. Please contact me to make arrangements for the transfer to occur.

Sincerely,

Attorney

_____, Inc.
Agent for_____ (Delaware)
Address

Re: Plaintiff v. Defendant
    Superior Court _____ County
    CAFN 12345A

Dear Sir/Madam:

    Enclosed is a Third-Party Request for Production of Documents directed to you as agent for service of process for _____, Inc. I believe the Request speaks for itself concerning the documents that are being sought, but feel free to call me if you have any questions.

    Although the Request requires delivery of the documents to my office within 31 days, copies of the documents may be produced, and I will be happy to make arrangements to have them delivered to my office. Please call me so that we may make arrangements convenient to you.

                Very truly yours,

                Attorney

Letter to Counsel for Third Party Re: Subpoena
for Production of Evidence

Ms. _____
Senior Administrative Paralegal
& Custodian of Records
A. _____ Brokerage

      Re: Subpoena for Production of Evidence at a Deposition
          Plaintiff v. Defendant
          Superior Court of ____ County
          CAFN 12345A

Dear Ms. _____:

Thank you for your letter of May 4, 2006, regarding the subpoena served in the above-referenced case. As you suggested, I will limit my request for documents to those generated on or after January 1, 2005. The monthly statements I am requesting include the following accounts: (a) account number 112235121; (b) account number 444555666; (c) account number 666555444; (d) account 222333444; (e) account number 999888777; and (f) account number 888777666.

It is my understanding that Mr. _____ is also custodian for his children with several accounts at your company. As we discussed on the telephone, the subpoena does not encompass those accounts. It does, however, include any accounts other than those listed in which Mr._____ has an interest.

Moreover, it is my understanding from your letter that we can expect to receive these documents in approximately two weeks. It is also my understanding that you will provide a cost estimate to me. If you have any questions, or if I may provide additional information, please let me know. Thank you for your assistance in this matter.

          Sincerely,

          Attorney

CHAPTER

8

Opposing Counsel
Address

Re: Plaintiff v. Defendant
    Superior Court of ＿＿＿ County
    CAFN 12345A

Dear (Opposing Counsel):

As you have requested, I have reviewed our Request for Production of Documents and am willing to limit the initial production to the documents and information as follows:

1. Corporate tax returns;

3. Personal income tax returns;

5. Pay and distribution information from December 31, 2005;

6. Banking information from December 31, 2005;

7. Title certificates, etc., for property acquired after December 31, 2005;

13. Information on insurance that was in force any time after December 31, 2005;

14. Information on any medical insurance that was in force after December 31, 2005;

21. I need this information.

22. Credit card information after December 31, 2005;

23. Documents that are responsive to this Request;

28. A Response.

I have agreed to limit the documents required by the first Request in order to aid your client in gathering the more important documents so that I can receive them in advance of the mediation scheduled June 1, 2006. 1 will expect to receive the remainder of the documents on or before May 2, 2006. I also assume that the Responses to Interrogatories will be served at the appropriate time. If I have been unclear or if you have any questions, please let me know.

Very truly yours,

Attorney

Opposing Counsel
Address

    Re: Plaintiff v. Defendant
        Superior Court of _____ County
        CAFN 12345A

Dear (Opposing Counsel):

    This letter will confirm our voicemail memos back and forth to each other concerning production of documents. It is my understanding that as of June 1, 2006, your client was to produce all of the documents requested pursuant to our Notice to Produce and Request for Production of Documents. It is my further understanding that he has not made contact with you in order to make this production possible. My client's documents are in my office and ready for your review upon our receipt or ability to review his documents.

    Because your client's documents are not available, we are unwilling to remove the Status Conference on Wednesday, June 28, 2006, before Judge _____, because we need to keep this case moving forward. Please call me if your client has his documents available so that we can proceed.

                          Very truly yours,

                          Attorney

Transmittal Letter to Opposing Counsel with Motion to Compel Discovery

Opposing Counsel
Address

  Re: Plaintiff v. Defendant
    Superior Court of ____ County
    CAFN 12345A

Dear (Opposing Counsel):

  Enclosed please find your service copies of the following:

- Plaintiff's Motion to Compel Responses to Discovery and for Sanctions w/Attachments

  - Certificate of Service re: Discovery
  - Plaintiffs First Request for Supplement by Defendant to Plaintiff's First Interrogatories, Notice to Produce, and Request for Production of Documents to Defendant
  - Plaintiff's First Interrogatories to Defendant
  - Plaintiff's First Notice to Produce to Defendant
  - Plaintiff's First Request for Production of Documents to Defendant

- Brief in Support of Plaintiff's Motion to Compel Responses to Discovery and for Sanctions
- Certification of Attempt to Resolve Discovery Dispute
- Certificate of Service re: Plaintiff's Motion to Compel Discovery and for Sanctions

  Should you have any questions regarding the foregoing, please do not hesitate to contact me.

       Very truly yours,

       Attorney

Transmittal Letter to Opposing Counsel with Discovery Objections

Opposing Counsel
Address

Re: Plaintiff v. Defendant
    Superior Court of _____ County
    CAFN 12345A

Dear (Opposing Counsel):

Enclosed please find the Plaintiff's Objections and Responses to Defendant's First Request for Production of Documents, Plaintiff's Objections and Responses to Defendant's First Interrogatories, and Certificates of Service in the above-referenced case.

As always, if you have any questions please feel free to call.

Very truly yours,

Attorney

Opposing Counsel
Address

Re: Plaintiff v. Defendant
Superior Court of _____ County
CAFN 12345A

Dear (Opposing Counsel):

I have been reviewing the _____ file in preparation for the hearing next Wednesday, the 16th, and, in particular, I was looking at your client's discovery responses. I am shocked and amazed to find that your client has yet to produce the first document to me. Please immediately forward documents that are responsive to Notice to Produce and Request for Production of Documents, especially numbers 5, 6, 13, 14, 19, 21, 22, 24, and 27. Please let me know when I can expect to receive these. Given your attitude expressed in your Motion to Compel recently filed, I will take great offense if you require me to come to your office to pick up these documents; however, if that is necessary, let me know immediately so that I can make the necessary arrangements.

Also, I have received your Notice of Deposition of a third party for Thursday, June 1, 2006, at 10:00 A.M. at your office, but I have heard from other sources that this deposition will not actually take place.

Please let me know immediately what your intentions are with regard to the Notice of Deposition to the custodian of records for _____ Corporation. I look forward to your early responses to these matters.

Sincerely,

Attorney

Depositions

Not all cases include depositions. Depositions often happen in cases where the degree of hostility is high, and it is important for you to remember this in order to prepare your client as much as possible ahead of time. You need your client's help in the preparation. You also need your client to be relatively clear-headed during the deposition to point out gaps and inconsistencies in the testimony of the deponent. It is a good idea to send your client not only the Notice of Deposition but also an explanation of how the deposition works. Clients are afraid of depositions; the court reporter, the wily opposing counsel, and, worst of all, the dreaded soon-to-be ex-spouse, whom your client may not have even seen since the separation. Some of the anxiety can be lessened with a soothing and informative letter, explaining how the process works in simple language. This is also a good place to include deposition tips, even though you will be reviewing those same tips with the client when you meet to prepare for the occasion. It is, of course, standard procedure to confirm the deposition with opposing counsel and the court reporter by letter. Finally, it helps to remember that more than one case has settled after the parties have been cooped up with each other all day exploring their marriage.

Letter to Client Re: Request of Opposing Counsel for Deposition

Client
Address

Re: Plaintiff v. Defendant
    Superior Court of _____ County
    CAFN 12345A

Dear (Client):

I had a call today from your spouse's attorney, who wants to take your deposition. We have tentatively scheduled the deposition for June 1, 2006, at 10:00 A.M. at my office. Please give me a call and let me know if this time is convenient for you.

As you may already know, a deposition is an opportunity for an attorney to gather information about the other party or from a potential witness in a case. We will take the deposition in my conference room. You and I will be there; your husband's lawyer, Mr._____, and probably your husband will be there; and a court reporter will be there. The court reporter will place you under oath and then Mr. _____ will ask you a series of questions. I would expect most of those questions to be about your income and expenses. He may have questions about various credit card charges, and he may ask how you arrived at various expense items listed on your Financial Affidavit. He may also ask you about your company benefits, your retirement plan, and other assets.

Everything that is said is taken down by the court reporter. After the deposition is over, he or she will transcribe what was said and send us a transcript. It will look something like a play script. You will have the opportunity to review it and make corrections, if necessary. You will then sign it as a true record of what you said.

I would like to meet with you sometime during the first part of next week so that we can discuss the deposition process in more detail. Mr. _____ would also like to review your bank statements during the deposition, so please gather them together and bring them with you to our planning session.

I do plan to take your spouse's deposition, but I do not want to do so until after I have received his discovery responses. However, it might be worthwhile to at least begin his deposition as soon as yours is completed. We will talk about the feasibility of this next week.

Please give me a call so that we can discuss this in detail. I look forward to talking with you.

Sincerely,

Attorney

Short Letter to Client Re: Request of Opposing Counsel for Deposition

Client
Address

Re: Plaintiff v. Defendant
    Superior Court of _____ County
    CAFN 12345A

Dear (Client):

I had a call today from your husband's attorney, who wants to take your deposition. We have tentatively scheduled it for June 1, 2006, at 10:00 A.M. at his office on Main Street. Please give me a call the first of the week so that we can discuss this. Your husband's attorney would also like to review your bank statements at that time. I do not want to take your husband's deposition until after I have received his discovery responses, but it might be worthwhile to at least start his deposition at the same time. We will talk about this next week.

Please give me a call.

Sincerely,

Attorney

Client
Address

Re: Plaintiff v. Defendant (insert style of case)
    Superior Court of _____ County
    CAFN 12345A

Dear (Client):

Enclosed are copies of the subpoenas I have received from your spouse's attorney for depositions on June 1, 2006. It appears that he will depose your mother and your two brothers that day, and he wants everyone in his office at 10:00 A.M. He also subpoenaed Dr. _____ for 10:00 A.M. that day, but it appears that Dr. _____ cannot be present at that time, so the good doctor's deposition is now set for Monday, June 5, at 4:30 P.M. I will talk with you sometime this week before I see you next Thursday morning.

                    Sincerely,

                    Attorney

CHAPTER

9

LETTERS FOR
DIVORCE
LAWYERS

Client
Address

Re: Plaintiff v. Defendant
Superior Court of _____ County
CAFN 12345A

Dear (Client):

Enclosed are several items:

1. The transcript of your deposition. Please read through this carefully and mark any misprints or typos that you see.

2. The original Errata Sheet. If the transcript needs to be changed in any way, please list those changes on the Errata Sheet, sign it, and have your signature notarized. Then, return the original to the court reporter and send a copy to me.

3. The bill for the depositions. Please pay this directly. I have a copy of the bill to include in your expenses of litigation. If you have any questions about this, of course, please let me know.

Sincerely,

Attorney

Court Reporter
Address

   Re: Plaintiff v. Defendant
       Superior Court of _____ County
       CAFN 12345A

Dear (Court Reporter):

   This letter is to confirm that you will take the deposition of the opposing party in the above-referenced case on June 1, 2006, at 10:00 A.M. at my office. It is my understanding that opposing counsel, Mr. _____, will also depose my client when his client's deposition is completed. I am enclosing copies of the Notices of Deposition for your records.

   If you have any questions, please let me know. Otherwise, I will see you June 1st.

                              Sincerely,

                              Attorney

Transmittal of Notice of Deposition to Opposing Counsel

Opposing Counsel
Address

Re: Plaintiff v. Defendant
      Superior Court of _____ County
      CAFN 12345A

Dear (Opposing Counsel):

Enclosed please find your service copy of our Notice of Deposition of your client, _____, and the Certificate of Service regarding same. Please notify this office immediately if this date/time is inconvenient to either you or your client.

Very truly yours,

Attorney

Opposing Counsel
Address

Re: Plaintiff v. Defendant
    Superior Court of _____ County
    CAFN 12345A

Dear (Opposing Counsel):

This letter is to confirm that we will meet in your office next Thursday, February 23, 2006, at 10:00 A.M. so that you can take the deposition of my client, _____. You will provide the court reporter.

Depending on the length of her deposition, I would like to begin the deposition of your client on subject areas other than financial matters, since I do not want to depose him on financial matters until after I have had an opportunity to review his documents and interrogatory responses. If you have no objection, I will plan to proceed as outlined.

Sincerely,

Attorney

Letter to Opposing Counsel in Response to Notice of Deposition

Opposing Counsel
Address

Re: Plaintiff v. Defendant
  Superior Court of _____ County
  CAFN 12345A

Dear (Opposing Counsel):

   I have received your Notice of Deposition of my client, _____, and have no objection to having it on December 8th.

   I would also like to take your client's deposition on that day. Enclosed is a Notice of Deposition for her for 1:00 P.M. that day.

                      Sincerely,

                      Attorney

Opposing Counsel
Address

Re: Plaintiff v. Defendant
    Superior Court of _____ County
    CAFN 12345A

Dear (Opposing Counsel):

This letter is to confirm that I will begin depositions in the above-referenced case at your office next Thursday, June 1, 2006, at 9:30 A.M. I will provide the court reporter. I will begin by deposing your client, _____, and expect his deposition to take more than one day. Please make sure he brings all of his documents with him, since I have numerous questions about them.

In addition, I would like to depose his secretary, _____, as well as his brother, _____, and his nephew, _____. In terms of scheduling, I have set aside June 1st, 2nd, and 5th for these depositions, and am concerned that we will not complete them within that time period. We will just have to see how it goes.

Also, I never received a direct response to my request that your client's condominium in _____ be made available for appraisal. We would like to take care of this as soon as possible

Thank you for your cooperation in this matter.

          Sincerely,

          Attorney

Letter to Opposing Counsel Confirming Several Depositions
Plus Other Matters

Opposing Counsel
Address

Re: Plaintiff v. Defendant
   Superior Court of _____ County
   CAFN 12345A

Dear (Opposing Counsel):

This letter will cover a number of miscellaneous items.

First, this will confirm that I will take the depositions of _____, _____, _____, and _____ at your office. I will begin with _____'s deposition at 1:30 P.M. on Tuesday, April 4, 2006. I plan to take the depositions in the order listed above and will plan to continue on April 5, 1995. Please have _____ bring all documents that are specified in the various Notices to Produce and Requests for Production of Documents. I will have at least one person with me who can review documents as the depositions proceed. You have agreed to provide the court reporter. It is also my understanding that you will make these witnesses available without the necessity of subpoenas.

Secondly, I need to make arrangements to evaluate various properties. How do you suggest we handle the mechanics of access to the properties by appraisers? We need an appraisal for the _____ Drive and _____ Ferry residences. We also need something on the _____ Road property. Did your client get a formal appraisal from the bank? In addition, we need appraisals on the rental properties.

Thirdly, I would like to have appraisals on the wine collection, gun collection, motorcycles, and Rolls-Royce. When will it be convenient to do these?

Finally, in addition to the documents listed on the third Notice to Produce that is enclosed, I have asked for many other documents that have been promised but not delivered. I am sure you can understand that the business and property dealings in this matter are complicated and appear to be poorly documented, and that I must do a thorough examination in order to properly serve my client. If you can get documents to me prior to April 1st, I hope that having the opportunity to review them before the depositions will cut down on the time necessary for me to depose your client and the others.

Thank you for your continued assistance. I look forward to hearing from you.

Sincerely,

Attorney

Transmittal Letter to Third Party (Bank) with Subpoena for the
Production of Evidence at a Deposition

_____ Bank, N.A.
Custodian of Records
c/o _____, Registered Agent
Address

Re: Plaintiff v. Defendant
Superior Court of _____ County
CAFN 12345A

Dear Sir or Madam:

Attached please find a Subpoena for the Production of Evidence at a
Deposition in the above-referenced matter. The documents and records
you are requested to produce are set out in the Subpoena itself.

Your attendance is not required if all records in your custody are
produced by the close of business on Thursday, November 17, 2006.

Sincerely,

Attorney

Transmittal Letter to Third Party (Credit Card Information) with
Subpoena for the Production of Evidence at a Deposition

CHAPTER

9

Depositions

_____ Bank
Custodian of Records
Address

Re: Plaintiff v. Defendant
    Superior Court of _____ County
    CAFN 12345A

    Card: Visa—Defendant _____
    Account Nos.: 0000-0000-0000-0000;1111-1111-1111-1111
    Card: MasterCard—Defendant_____
    Account Nos.: 0000-0000-0000-0000; 1111-1111-1111-1111

To whom it may concern:

Attached please find a Subpoena for the Production of Evidence at a
Deposition in the above-referenced matter. The documents and records
you are notified and requested to produce are set out in the Subpoena
itself.

It is possible that some of these records will be more readily acces-
sible than others. In the event it is impossible to produce all subpoenaed
records by the date of the deposition, please produce all of those that are
available by that time. If there is any question about which documents
to produce, please call me.

Your attendance is not required if all records in your custody are
produced by the close of business on Wednesday, September 6, 2006.

Sincerely,

Attorney

Transmittal Letter to Opposing Counsel Objecting to Third-Party
Deposition Subpoena

Opposing Counsel
Address

Re: Plaintiff v. Defendant
    Superior Court of _____ County
    CAFN 12345A

Dear (Opposing Counsel):

It is my understanding that the deposition called for by the subpoena
to ____ Brokerage Co. for May 8th will not be held. I have not been
served with a copy of the subpoena as filed, but only received a copy of
a subpoena for deposition through the deponent. Please provide me with
copies of any future subpoenas.

As a precaution, I enclose herewith Objections. These Objections
relate to any account with _____ Brokerage in which my client is
trustee and also to his holdings prior to his marriage.

My client informs me that his wife will not give him his passport. I
see no reason for her to withhold this from him and request that you
advise her to return it to him.

With kindest personal regards, permit me to remain

                                        Very truly yours,

                                        Attorney

Response to Opposing Counsel and Objection to Third-Party Subpoena
for the Production of Medical Evidence at a Deposition

CHAPTER

9

Depositions

Opposing Counsel
Address

Re: Plaintiff v. Defendant
Superior Court of _____ County
CAFN 12345A

Dear (Opposing Counsel):

I received copies of your subpoenas to _____ Hospital and
_____, M.D., which provide in part, "Your attendance is not
required if all records in your custody are produced to our office by the
close of business at 5:00 P.M., on May 12, 2006."

This type of subpoena directly violates Standard 4 of the Disciplinary Rules. First, there has been no notice of deposition filed and served upon me, and, in fact, no deposition has been scheduled. Although I was served with a copy of the subpoena, that is not sufficient to meet the requirements of the standards for the Disciplinary Rules. Second, the subpoenas to the medical providers were misleading and could convince a non-party witness to divulge confidential and privileged information without my client first having an opportunity to contest the relevancy, confidentiality, or privilege of material contained in the files, because the subpoenas were sent without proper notice and with improper instructions.

Please contact me so that we may discuss this matter directly.

Very truly yours,

Attorney

Letter from Attorney for Third-Party Corporation
Regarding Discovery Subpoena

Attorney for Plaintiff
Address

Attorney for Defendant
Address

Re: Plaintiff v. Defendant
Superior Court of _____ County
CAFN 12345A

Dear Counsel:

As you are aware, this firm represents _____ Corporation. On May 1, 2006, Plaintiff's attorney issued a Notice of Deposition to my client, _____ Co., on behalf of the Plaintiff, together with a subpoena requesting the production of certain e-mails generated to or from Defendant, _____, a _____ Co. employee. On May 2, 2006, 1 spoke with Plaintiff's counsel and told him that, notwithstanding the over-breadth of the subpoena, the Company would need additional time to determine whether, *technologically speaking*, it is even feasible to obtain any of the requested data. In order to give the Company additional time to review the technological feasibility of obtaining any such records, Mr. ____ agreed to postpone the deposition and said that the subpoenaed documents did not need to be provided by the June 1, 2006, date indicated. I received written confirmation from his office Monday that the deposition and scheduled time for production of documents has been postponed, with no definitive reschedule date.

In my conversation with him regarding the Notice and subpoena, I pointed out that in its present form, the subpoena is objectionable on numerous grounds. For instance, the subpoena is not limited as to time and is overbroad in scope, inasmuch as it requests e-mail transmissions that are confidential, proprietary, and otherwise privileged. In that conversation, he said that it was not his intention to obtain any business-related e-mails, and he further said that he would consider methods for further limiting the scope of the subpoena, and in particular he would determine whether there are any specific individuals with whom Plaintiff believes Defendant may have communicated by e-mail that would be relevant to the underlying litigation, On Tuesday, he called and told me that he does not want any e-mails sent to or received from anybody with an e-mail address ending in "@__.com."

Late Tuesday we received a telephone call from Defendant's counsel, Ms. ____, who told me that the Defendant had filed a Motion for Protective Order, a copy of which she faxed to me. We have not yet received any response on behalf of the Plaintiff, nor have we received any indication from the Court as to its position on these matters.

Today, I received some additional information from my client regarding the technological feasibility of obtaining Defendant's e-mails. It is my understanding that Defendant uses a Company-issued laptop computer with a docking station. I understand that his computer would have provided weekly postings and backups to the Company's central computer server. I also understand that the main server provided monthly backup data, which is stored and maintained by an outside company off-site. This third party retains the backup data on a one-year "rolling basis," meaning that, at any particular time, only data from the previous one-year period is, in theory, obtainable. All such data is permanently deleted after a year. Therefore, in theory, the Company could access certain of Defendant's e-mail records from the past one-year period.

Notwithstanding the above, the burden of reviewing this data and presenting it in a non-objectionable form will be substantial. All of the data will need to be reviewed to exclude any confidential, proprietary or privileged information. Limiting the search to messages to or from persons without an "@_____.com" address will not be of much help, because many of the Company's employees and clients who regularly exchange confidential messages with Defendant have different types of e-mail addresses. Because Defendant is a high-ranking executive in the Company and regularly receives and disseminates highly confidential data, the Company will have to appoint another high-level person to cull through the messages to determine which ones are non-objectionable and producible. Furthermore, we anticipate that it would take Company personnel approximately ten (10) days to two (2) weeks to review the literally thousands of documents to determine which would be producible. Before the Company undertakes that obligation, we would need to obtain a firm Agreement with counsel for the Defendant and the Plaintiff concerning the payment for the costs to be incurred in such an undertaking. If an agreement cannot be reached as to the payment of such costs, we will have no alternative but to seek Court intervention to quash or modify the subpoena, for Georgia law recognizes that if a subpoena is oppressive or unreasonable, a Court may condition production of the requested documents upon the advancement by the person on whose behalf the subpoena was issued of the reasonable cost of producing the requested documentary evidence.

Please be assured that the Company fully intends to comply with all applicable provisions of Georgia law and will abide by any obligations to produce the subpoenaed records on reasonable terms. In light of the fact that the Defendant's Motion for Protective Order is pending, we do not think it would be appropriate for the Company to provide any documents until the Court has ruled on the issue.

If the matters addressed above are incorrect or contrary to your understanding of the status of this matter, please contact me immediately. I look forward to speaking with you again soon.

Sincerely,

Attorney for _____ Co.

Scheduling Various Pretrial Matters

ometimes it seems like half your time is spent coordinating and scheduling things. Even though you may have talked with everyone involved during the process, confirm it in writing!

Letter to Clerk Requesting Information
for Filing Complaint in Local Court

Clerk of _____ Court
Address

Dear (Clerk):

    I anticipate filing a Complaint for Divorce in the Superior Court of _____ County shortly after the first of the year. In connection with the above, would you please forward specific documents and/or instructions for the filing of a Complaint for Divorce in _____ County in the envelope enclosed?

    Thank you for your assistance in this matter.

                Sincerely,

                Attorney

Letter to Judge's Secretary to Confirm That
Hearing Has Been Scheduled

_____

Secretary to Judge _____
_____ County Superior Court

    Re: Plaintiff v. Defendant
        Superior Court of _____ County
        CAFN 12345A

Dear (Secretary):

    This letter is to confirm that the above-referenced case has been set down for a temporary hearing as a back-up case for the week of May 29, 2006. If the case is not reached that week, then it is specially set for June 19, 2006. Please let me know if you have any questions. Thank you very much for your assistance

                  Very truly yours,

                  Attorney

Letter to Judge's Secretary Requesting Case
Be Stipulated to Trial Calendar

_____

Secretary to Judge _____
_____ County Superior Court

    Re: Plaintiff v. Defendant
       Superior Court of _____ County
       CAFN 12345A

Dear (Secretary):

    Per our telephone conversation today, this is to request that you stipulate the above-referenced domestic matter to Judge _____'s next available Civil Jury Trial Calendar. By copy of this letter I am notifying opposing counsel, _____, of this request. Your cooperation in this matter is greatly appreciated.

    If you have questions concerning any of the foregoing, please do not hesitate to contact me.

                  Sincerely,

                  Attorney

Letter to Judge to Remove Case from One Calendar and Specially Set on Another

Honorable _____
Judge of _____ Court
Address

     Re: Plaintiff v. Defendant
        Superior Court of _____ County
        CAFN 12345A

Dear Judge _____:

    Please have your calendar clerk remove the above-referenced case from your June 1, 2006, calendar and specially set it for 10:00 A.M. on Tuesday, June 20, 2006. 1 have consulted with Plaintiff's counsel, who informs me that she is available that day and has authorized me to add her consent to this letter.

    Please let me know if you have any questions. Thank you for your assistance in this matter.

                  Sincerely,

                  Attorney

10

Letter to Remove Case from Calendar Because of Leave of Absence

_____, Case Manager to
The Honorable _____
_____ Superior Court
Address

Re: Plaintiff v. Defendant
    Superior Court of _____County
    CAFN 12345A

Dear (Case Manager):

I have received notice that the (case name) case is scheduled for a 120-Day Status Conference on Thursday, June 1, 2006. Please be advised that I have a leave of absence that includes that date. In addition, not only does opposing counsel have a conflict, but the parties are also doing some work with a counselor, which might facilitate the ultimate settlement of this matter. At this point, I do not believe a Conference will help, so I am requesting that you remove this case from the Judge's calendar for June 1st.

If you have any questions or if I may provide additional information, please let me know. Thank you for your assistance in this matter.

Very truly yours,

Attorney

Letter to Clerk Confirming that Case Has Been Removed from One Calendar and Placed on Another

_____
Deputy Court Clerk
_____ County Superior Court
Address

      Re: Plaintiff v. Defendant
          Superior Court of _____ County
          CAFN 12345A

Dear (Deputy Court Clerk):

    This letter is to confirm our telephone conversation of June 1 2006, that the above-referenced case has been removed from Judge _____'s June 9, 2006, temporary hearing calendar and has been reset to Judge _____'s July 6, 2006, calendar. We will appear for that calendar at 9:30 A.M. unless the parties are able to reach a temporary resolution of matters before then. Thank you for your assistance in this matter.

                Sincerely,

                Attorney

Letter to Judge's Secretary Specially Setting Case for Trial

_____

Secretary to Judge _____
____ County Superior Court
Address

        Re: Plaintiff v. Defendant
           Superior Court of ____ County
           CAFN 12345A

Dear (Secretary):

    This letter is to confirm our conversation today during which the above-referenced case was removed from the back-up calendar for the weeks of May 29, 2006 and June 12, 2006, and reset for a two-day bench trial beginning July 11, 2006. By copy of this letter I am notifying _____, opposing counsel, of these changes. Thank you for your assistance in this matter.

                    Very truly yours,

                    Attorney

Letter to Court Asking for Continuance Because of Temporary Settlement

BY FACSIMILE ONLY
  (000) 000-0000
Honorable _____
Judge of _____Court
Address

　　　Re: Plaintiff v. Defendant
　　　　　Superior Court of _____ County
　　　　　CAFN 12345A

Dear Judge _____:

　　　The above-referenced case is scheduled for a 60-Day Status Conference at 3:00 P.M. today. Both parties would greatly appreciate it if the Conference could be postponed. The reasons for this request are that the parties have already had a 30-day meeting with Ms. ____; the parties have reached a temporary agreement and will submit a proposed temporary order to the Court shortly; and the parties are in the process of discovery so that they can work on a settlement.

　　　Accordingly, on behalf of both parties and their counsel, I respectfully request that the Status Conference, scheduled for later today, be postponed. Thank you for your cooperation and assistance in this matter.

　　　　　　　　　　　Sincerely,

　　　　　　　　　　　Attorney

Letter to Court Asking for Continuance Because of Illness

BY FACSIMILE ONLY
(000) 000-0000

Honorable _____
Judge of _____ Court
Address

      Re: Plaintiff v. Defendant
          Superior Court of _____ County
          CAFN 12345A

Dear Judge _____:

    Please accept this correspondence as a request for a continuance in the above-referenced matter, which is scheduled for jury trial on Thursday, June 1, 2006. The reason for this request is the Defendant's attorney has been very ill for the past few days and has not been able to prepare for this trial, nor do we anticipate him being well enough to appear for trial. Opposing counsel has been informed of his status since early yesterday and has no objection to the continuance.

    Please consider this request and notify us at your earliest convenience so that witnesses can be released as soon as possible

                 Very truly yours,

                 Legal Assistant to Attorney
                 for the Firm

Letter Notifying Court that Attorney No Longer Represents Client

_____, Case Manager to
The Honorable _____
_____ Superior Court
Address

> Re: Plaintiff v. Defendant
> Superior Court of _____ County
> CAFN 12345A

Dear (Case Manager):

I have received notice that the above-referenced case is scheduled for a 60-Day Status Conference on Thursday, June 1, 2006, at 10:00 A.M. Please be advised that this firm no longer represents (former client). (New attorney) is now (former client's) new counsel.

If you have any questions, or if I may provide additional information, please let me know. Thank you for your assistance in this matter.

Very truly yours,

Attorney

Letter to Judge Requesting Continuance Because of a Leave of Absence

Honorable _____
Judge of _____Court
Address

    Re: Plaintiff v. Defendant
       Superior Court of _____ County
       CAFN 12345-A

Dear Judge _____:

    I represent the Defendant, Mr._____ in the above-referenced case, and have contacted _____, counsel for Plaintiff, in an attempt to reschedule the Petition Seeking Relief From Family Violence hearing scheduled for June 5, 2006, at 9:00 A.M., as I have a leave of absence scheduled during this period that will not end until June 16, 2006.

    As the enclosed copy of my letter to opposing counsel indicates, I have asked that she reschedule the hearing after June 16, 2006, as I will be in _____, Tennessee, on that date to enter a criminal plea before the Honorable_____, United States District Judge. The case there is *United States v.*_____, Indictment No. CR-122345A.

    If opposing counsel does not voluntarily agree to reschedule, I am requesting that you continue this hearing. A Temporary Protective Order is in effect against my client, and he is also in federal custody at this time. I do not know whether he will be released on bond prior to the June 5th hearing date. Thus, opposing counsel cannot show that any harm will occur from delaying this hearing until after June 16, 2006.

    Your cooperation in this matter is greatly appreciated. If you have any questions, please do not hesitate to contact my office, as I will be in periodic contact with my secretary during my leave of absence.

                    With kindest regards,

                    Attorney

Letter to Judge Objecting to Opposing Counsel's Request for Continuance

Honorable _____
Judge of _____Court
Address

Re: Plaintiff v. Defendant
      Superior Court of _____ County
      CAFN 12345A

Dear Judge _____:

I have received a copy of opposing counsel's letter requesting that the hearing in the above-referenced case, now scheduled for June 5, 2006, be postponed until after June 16, 2006. 1 cannot agree to this continuance. First of all, this petition was filed May 8, 2006, and the Protective Order will expire June 8, 2006.

Second, while opposing counsel may have leave of absence in other cases, she does not have one in this case. My understanding of the rule is that she has the option to accept or decline a new case when a hearing date falls during a planned trip, but leaves of absence in other cases do not offer protection in the new case.

Finally, this is the second petition I have filed for my client this spring. We were unable to have a hearing on the first petition because we did not get service on the Defendant. My client is anxious to be heard in this matter and does not want to run the risk that the Ex Parte Protective Order will lapse before she gets to Court. For these reasons, I am asking the Court to deny opposing counsel's request and permit this matter to go forward on June 5, 2006, as now scheduled.

Thank you for your assistance in this matter.

        Sincerely,

        Attorney

Conflict Letter When You Have to Be in More Than One Place
at the Same Time

The Honorable S. _____
Judge, ____ Superior Court

The Honorable H. _____
Judge, ____ Superior Court

RE: Potential Conflict for Thursday, June 1, 2006

Dear Judges:

This letter is written in compliance with Rule 17.1 of the Uniform Superior Court Rules to notify the Court of a potential conflict for the day referenced above.

I certify that I am lead counsel in all the cases listed below and that these matters cannot be adequately handled nor the clients' interest adequately protected by other attorneys in this firm.

Thursday, June 1, 2006 at 9:00 A.M.

Case # 1:   Plaintiff v. Defendant
                 _____ Superior Court—Final Hearing
                 CAFN 12345A
                 Opposing Counsel: _____, Esq.
                 P.O. Box XXX
                 _____, Georgia

Thursday, June 1, 2006 at 9:30 A.M.

Case # 2   Plaintiff v. Defendant
                 _____ Superior Court—Contempt
                 CAFN 22221A
                 Opposing Counsel: _____, Esq.
                 Twenty-First Floor
                 xxx Road
                 _____, Georgia

Thursday, June 1, 2006, at 2:00 P.M.

Case # 3:   Plaintiff v. Defendant
_____ Superior Court—Mediation
CAFN 44441A
Opposing Counsel: _____, Esq.
One Center, Suite 2
1 _____ Street
_____, Georgia

Mediator: _____, Esq.
_____ Avenue
_____, Georgia

1 am on trial in Case # 1 and this will be the second day of the trial. I anticipate completing this case on Thursday afternoon. Therefore, I will report to Case # 1 first. Should that case settle or finish June 1st, I will report for Case # 2 as soon as possible. In the event both cases are resolved by 2:00 P.M., I will report for the scheduled mediation in Case # 3.

If the above is not acceptable, please contact my office with instructions and order of appearance. Thanking you in advance for your cooperation, I am,

Very truly yours,

Attorney

Cc: Ms. _____, Secretary for Judge S.
Ms. _____, Secretary for Judge K.
Clerk, _____ Superior Court

CHAPTER

10

LETTERS FOR
DIVORCE
LAWYERS

Notice of Leave of Absence

Practice tip. If your court system uses leaves of absence, always include the Friday preceding your vacation and the Monday following your vacation in your leave in order to protect your travel plans and peace of mind. This protects you from missing a flight Friday because of a hearing that goes too long or from coming back Sunday night with a case scheduled for trial the following Monday. Plan ahead and file your Notice as soon as you know when you will be gone.

Letter to Clerk for Leave of Absence

_____, Clerk
_____ County Superior Court
Address

      Re: Plaintiff v. Defendant
      CAFN E-11111

      Plaintiff v. Defendant
      CAFN E-22222

      Plaintiff v. Defendant
      CAFN E-33333

      Plaintiff v. Defendant
      CAFN E-44444

Dear (Clerk):

Enclosed please find my Application for Leave of Absence in the above-referenced cases. I anticipate being out of town from June 1 through June 14, 2006.

I would appreciate your returning a date-stamped copy in the enclosed envelope.

Thank you for your assistance in this matter.

                  Sincerely,

                  Attorney

Notice of Leave of Absence

TO: All Judges, Clerks of Court and Counsel of Record

FROM: (Attorney)_____, Esquire

RE: Notice of Leave of Absence

DATE: April 5, 2006

COMES NOW, (Attorney)_____, Esq. and respectfully notifies all Judges before whom she has cases pending, all affected clerks of court, and all opposing counsel that she will be on leave pursuant to Georgia Uniform Code Rule 16.

The period of leave during which time applicant shall be away from the practice of law is:

Friday, June 2, 2006, through and including Monday, June 12, 2006.

All affected Judges and opposing counsel shall have ten (10) days from the date of this Notice to make objection. If no objections are filed, the leave shall be granted.

RESPECTFULLY SUBMITTED, this _____ day of April 2006.

Temporary Matters

All sorts of things happen between the time the client becomes a client and the time the case is completed. There may be discovery, temporary hearings, various motions, and negotiations. The discovery matters are handled in another section of this book devoted exclusively to them. This section includes letters for some of the other matters that come up.

Letter to Judge Asking that a Judge from Another Circuit Be Appointed

The Honorable _____, Judge
Superior Court of _____ County
Address

      Re: Plaintiff v. Defendant
      CAFN 12345A

Dear (Judge):

    It is my understanding that all of the _____ County Superior Court Judges have recused themselves in this case because the Defendant practices law in this county. After consulting with my client, I would like to request that Judge _____ from _____ County be appointed to preside over this case, if he is willing. Opposing counsel, _____, concurs with this request. Thank you for your assistance in handling this matter.

                    Sincerely,

                    Attorney

Letter to Newly Appointed Judge

Honorable _____(Judge)
Chief Judge
Address

    Re: Plaintiff v. Defendant
       CAFN 12345A

Dear (Judge):

    Thank you for agreeing to preside over this case. I look forward to meeting with you and opposing counsel on Thursday, June 1, 2006, at 11:00 A.M. in Room 2 of the _____ County Courthouse.

               Sincerely,

               Attorney

Letter Notifying Judge that Contempt Matter Has Been Resolved

Honorable _____
Chief Judge
Address

Re: Plaintiff v. Defendant
    CAFN 12345A

Dear (Judge):

Since the Motion to Compel was filed, Mr. _____ has produced the requested documents. As a result, there is no need for a hearing June 1, 2006, at 1:30 P.M. on Plaintiff's Motion to Compel. If you would have your clerk remove this from your calendar, I would be most appreciative. If you have any questions, please let me know.

Sincerely,

Attorney

Letter to Opposing Counsel with Problems

CHAPTER

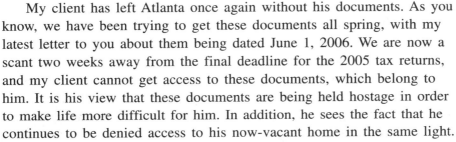

Temporary Matters

Opposing Counsel
Address

    Re: Plaintiff v. Defendant
        CAFN 12345A

Dear (Opposing Counsel):

    My client has left Atlanta once again without his documents. As you know, we have been trying to get these documents all spring, with my latest letter to you about them being dated June 1, 2006. We are now a scant two weeks away from the final deadline for the 2005 tax returns, and my client cannot get access to these documents, which belong to him. It is his view that these documents are being held hostage in order to make life more difficult for him. In addition, he sees the fact that he continues to be denied access to his now-vacant home in the same light.

    My client is also extremely upset by the fact that his counterproposal for settlement was sent to you April 1, and to date there has been no reply. The fact that there are so many things unsettled certainly exacerbates the state of his mental health.

    (Client) has directed that I inform you that his April 1 counterproposal is rescinded as of 5:00 P.M., Thursday, June 15, 2006, unless a written acceptance and his documents are received in my office prior to that time. Please be advised that when I say, "his documents," I mean all documents within those several boxes at your office that are either personal to him or joint accounts. We are not asking for anything that is strictly in your client's name or that belongs to ABC Company, but everything else should be delivered here.

    I hope we are able to move things along so that we can reach a speedy resolution. There are a number of problems quickly upcoming that will have to be addressed if we cannot reach a final resolution. I look forward to hearing from you.

                      Very truly yours,

                      Attorney

Letter Confirming Client Is Coming to Marital Residence
to Retrieve Items

Opposing Counsel
Address

Re: Plaintiff v. Defendant
     CAFN 12345A

Dear (Opposing Counsel):

This will confirm our agreement that my client, _____,
will come to the marital residence at 10:00 A.M. on Saturday, June 17,
2006, to retrieve various personal belongings from the home. As we
discussed, in addition to clothing, toiletries, and various personal items,
my client will get the keys to the car that your client does not want to
drive (either the _____ or the _____), the key to his personal mailbox,
and his personal lap-top computer. He will also need access to the
storage shed behind the house.

Furthermore, in order to enable us to move as swiftly as possible
regarding the finances of this marriage and the tax liability, my client
will need to retrieve various documents that are located in the home.

Thank you for your cooperation in this matter, and I look forward to
meeting with you next week.

Sincerely,

Attorney

_____, Judge
Address

    Re: Plaintiff v. Defendant
       CAFN 12345A

Dear (Judge):

    Recently I sent a letter to the Parenting Coordinator, _____, waiving my client's right to review her final report or to call her as a witness. I did this at her request, assuming that opposing counsel would do likewise. However, I have neither seen nor heard anything from him and assume that he did not enter a similar waiver on behalf of his client. It goes without saying that my waiver on behalf of my client is contingent upon opposing counsel's waiver on behalf of his client. If that waiver is not forthcoming, then I formally assert my right to receive a copy of any report that will be sent to the Court by the Parenting Coordinator, Ms. _____, and I reserve the right to call her as a witness. Thank you for your consideration of this matter.

                        Respectfully yours,

                        Attorney

Three Letters to Court Summarizing Closing Arguments for Parties After
Temporary Modification Hearing

Please note: Dates and figures do not necessarily follow any logical
pattern.

1. Letter on Behalf of Defendant Arguing Why a Temporary Reduction
in Support for Plaintiff Should Be Denied

Honorable _____, Judge
Superior Court of _____ County
Address

> Re: Plaintiff v. Defendant
> Superior Court of _____ County
> CAFN 12345-A

Dear Judge _____:

As you know, because of time constraints, opposing counsel and I
were unable to make closing arguments following the close of evidence
in the _____ temporary modification hearing. With the Court's
indulgence, I would like to take a few moments to summarize the
evidence as I see it.

O.C.G.A. § 19-6-19 authorizes a modification of alimony if the
petitioner convincingly shows a significant decrease in his income and
in his ability to pay his Court-ordered obligation. However, the statute
does not mandate a modification even if the petitioner does show a
significant change in his financial circumstances.

Among other factors the Court should consider at a temporary
hearing is the reasonable probability that the petitioner will prevail at the
final hearing. Unless the former husband ("Husband") suffers a change
more significant than what he presented at the temporary hearing, I do
not believe he has a reasonable probability of obtaining relief at the final
hearing. Consequently, he should not obtain any relief on a temporary
basis.

To begin with, Husband's income through October 31 of this year is
$60,000 (Exhibit D-2). If his income is annualized over 12 months, he
will earn over $72,000. It is obvious that the parties contemplated he
would pay $18,000 per year in alimony if his income was at that level.

Per the divorce agreement, Husband pays an additional 15 percent alimony if his gross income exceeds $50,000 (P-1, p. 8). While Husband testified that he earned $89,000 the year of the divorce, 2001, the former wife ("Wife") testified that her settlement was based on an assumed income of $75,000-$80,000. It is not likely that she would have agreed to alimony of $18,000 if she had known that his income was approaching $90,000. Husband's January 3, 2001, Financial Affidavit (D-4) and the March 1, 2001, letter written by Wife's attorney are certainly consistent with Wife's testimony that she had no idea he was earning so much money in 2001. In fact, she testified that on October 14, 2001, she signed both the 2000 joint income tax return and the Separation Agreement. She testified that the 2000 return was the last information she had about his income before the divorce was granted.

Regardless of his gross income, it is undisputed that Husband's ability to pay his alimony obligation has vastly improved in the years since the divorce. In 2001, he was the sole support for both children and himself. One child was in high school and the other in college. Husband later paid all college expenses for both children. Husband lived in and paid for a rented apartment and rented furniture. Husband had his legal fees and a $5,000 debt for Wife's legal fees. According to his 2001 Financial Affidavit, he owed $12,468 for 2000 taxes (D-4) and, according to his 2001 income tax return (P-2), he owed additional taxes of $15,323 for 2001 when he filed that return.

In contrast, today Husband is married and lives in a home owned and paid for by his current wife. Both of his children have completed their college educations and Husband has paid Wife's legal fees from the divorce. In the years since the divorce, Husband has, as well, earned substantial income. His taxes and alimony obligations total less than one half of his earnings and, as he himself testified, he lives a very conservative lifestyle—even driving the same automobile he had at the time of the divorce.

Given these facts, the key question becomes: Where has the rest of his money gone? What has he done with the money left over each month after his taxes, alimony, and retirement are subtracted? There is no evidence at all to explain why Husband's ability to pay his alimony has not significantly improved. At best, Husband has seriously mismanaged his income and credit, and there is at least some evidence to suggest that his income may have been lost through gambling.

Whatever the true story, Husband is now asking the Court to require Wife to indirectly pay his debts, even though paragraph 14 of the Settlement Agreement provides that "Husband and Wife shall not at any time hereafter contract any debts, obligations, or other liabilities whatsoever for which the other or his or her property or estate shall become or may become liable or answerable." But reducing Wife's alimony so that Husband can pay his creditors is doing just that.

Before Wife suffers any reduction, it might be appropriate for Husband to stop spending $2,500 monthly on his adult children; to reduce his $900 per month food expense; to ask his current wife to resume paying the utilities for her home; to ask his current wife, now retired with a pension, to pay for the weekly maid. Husband's alimony obligation to Wife is the only obligation he now has that is Court-ordered. Certainly his <u>legal</u> obligation should take precedence over those he sees as his <u>moral</u> obligations.

Based on the evidence presented to this Court, Husband is not entitled to a temporary reduction in his obligation, and we respectfully ask the Court to deny his motion. We also ask the Court to award attorneys' fees for Wife.

Thank you for your consideration of this issue, which is of vital importance to my client. As always, I appreciate the patience and attention to the parties that this Court gives in these matters.

Very truly yours,

Attorney for Defendant

2. Letter Summarizing Closing Argument for Plaintiff and Rebutting Defendant's Closing Argument

Honorable _____
Judge of ____ Court

Re: Plaintiff v. Defendant
    Superior Court of _____ County
    CAFN 12345-A

Dear (Judge):

I am in receipt of the letter to you from opposing counsel dated _____.

Inasmuch as Defendant's counsel has now argued her case, I feel compelled to respond and show the Court there indeed should be a temporary modification of the alimony award until the time of trial. The evidence clearly shows that there have been such changed circumstances of the parties since the Final Judgment and Decree that there is a reasonable probability that the Plaintiff will obtain revision upon final trial.

O.C.G.A. § 19-6-19(c) provides that in determining whether there should be a temporary modification, the Court should consider evidence of any changed circumstances of the parties and the reasonable probability of the petitioner obtaining revision upon final trial.

O.C.G.A. § 19-6-19(a) provides that the issue for determination in a modification of alimony action is whether there has been a change in the income and financial status of <u>either</u> former spouse since the Final Judgment and Decree. The evidence adduced at the hearing demonstrates that both Husband's income and financial status has drastically decreased, while on the other hand, Wife's income and financial status has dramatically increased since the Final Judgment and Decree was entered in 2001.

A. HUSBAND'S INCOME
The parties were divorced in November 2001, when Husband's earned income was $89,000. Now the evidence is that through October 31 of this year he has earned approximately $60,000, and it has been projected by his employer that Husband's gross income for this year will be approximately $72,000. (See Employer Affidavit, Plaintiff Exhibit 10.)

This decrease amounts to a significant reduction from his 2001 income. These facts represent not only a substantial reduction, but a drastic reduction, and as a result, Husband has been totally unable to meet his obligations.

In addition, the affidavit of the Employer as well as Husband's testimony reveal that his percentage participation in company profits has decreased from 13-15 percent in 2001 to 9.25 percent this year. Additional new partners in the company and a reevaluation of Husband's contribution to the company have accounted for this decrease in his percentage participation in the net profits.

B. HUSBAND'S FINANCIAL STATUS

Husband's 2000 Domestic Relations Financial Affidavit showed that his total debts at that time equaled $20,000 as compared to his present total debts of $60,000, as shown on his current Domestic Relations Financial Affidavit (Plaintiff's Exhibit 5). This represents an increase of $30,000 in his debt. As shown by his current affidavit and his testimony, well over half of this debt is because of monies due on present and past federal and state income tax obligations. Because of the extent of these obligations, with every day that passes, significant penalties and interest are added. This results in an inability to keep current with his obligations. In view of these facts, for the Wife to now argue that there has been a betterment of Husband's financial status during this period of time is simply ridiculous.

Husband has testified that he uses all of his income to pay not only his living expenses but past-due taxes, interest, and penalties on past-due taxes, as well as interest on numerous advances he has had to take on various credit cards in order to attempt to reduce his tax and other obligations. After these sums are paid out of his income, he has insufficient funds to even pay for things like new clothes or vacations. He is not able to accumulate any savings or purchase stocks or bonds, and his retirement fund has been substantially depleted because he has had to secure early withdrawal of retirement monies in order to pay past-due income taxes and other obligations. Further, as shown by his affidavit and testimony, Husband has no assets to sell to reduce these debts.

C. WIFE'S FINANCIAL STATUS

A comparison of Wife's 2001 Financial Affidavit (Plaintiff's Exhibit 9) as compared to her current Affidavit, combined with her testimony at the hearing, reveals that there has been a dramatic increase in her financial status since the Final Judgment and Decree. The evidence revealed that Wife's assets have significantly increased over that period of time. She testified that the value of her IRA alone had increased from $25,000 in 2001 to $82,000 now. With the alimony payments made by Husband, she has been able to contribute $2,000 to her IRA each and every year since the divorce. The evidence reveals that in 2001 her only other assets were her home and furniture, a car with no equity, no stocks and bonds, jewelry, cash value of life insurance, and no money in the bank. Now her home has increased in value, the mortgage has been reduced to just $18,000, and the cash value of her life insurance has increased from $32,500 to $48,200. Further, Wife has been bequeathed jewelry from her mother's estate that she does not even list in her current Domestic Relations Financial Affidavit. Although she admits that she is a beneficiary of her mother's estate, she claims that she does not have any idea what is in the estate other than the jewelry, although she states in her Domestic Relations Financial Affidavit on page 5 that she pays an attorney to represent her with respect to her mother's estate matters at a cost of $324 a month. Her affidavit, on page 5, also lists as a monthly expense income taxes that she has to pay on alimony payments in the amount of $1,924.08 per month. However, her 2004 federal and state income tax returns (Plaintiff's Exhibit 8) reveal that her actual tax for <u>all</u> her income was only $11,829 in federal and $3,033 in state taxes, or $1,222 per month. This is a misstatement of her actual expenses.

In addition to the above facts, the evidence revealed that, although Wife had no stocks in her own name at the time of the divorce, she has now amassed over $20,000 in stocks and bonds, the purchase of which was financed mainly through her alimony payments. Since the divorce, she has been able to accumulate over $20,000 from alimony payments and placed this in a savings account. Testimony further revealed that she spent significant amounts of money over the last several years for cosmetic surgery from amounts saved from alimony. She further testified that she has already received in excess of $32,000 from her mother's estate for the sale of her one-half (1/2) interest in her mother's condominium.

D. WIFE'S INCOME

Wife testified, and her tax returns reveal, that over the last three (3) years, she earned approximately $6,000 a year working only two or three days a week. Now, at the time of the hearing, she says she has just become unemployed. Further, she testified that she has not even tried to obtain permanent employment, and has made no application for such employment since the divorce.

E. OTHER COMMENTS

In response to opposing counsel's contention that Husband has $6,000 per month after his taxes, alimony, and retirement are subtracted, suffice it to say that counsel overlooks the following:

1. In addition to the alimony payments Husband pays, he is obligated to pay <u>non-modifiable</u> payments currently in the amount of $200 per month on an equity credit line and $300 per month for Wife's medical expenses. Originally, after the divorce, his payments on the equity line were as high as $1,000 per month. Further, such a statement does not take into consideration the thousands of dollars Husband has had to spend to support his children through college and, in the case of one of them, through medical school. In addition, it is anticipated that the other child will be attending graduate school while the first one completes medical school this coming year. Importantly, Husband's escalating penalties and interest have also not been considered.

Husband simply does not have any money left after the payment of alimony, his taxes, and retirement funds. The Court's attention is directed to his Financial Affidavit, which lists in meticulous detail where all his income is spent. After all expenses are paid, he is left with a huge monthly deficit, as his monthly payment to creditors of $2,000 does not even take into account most of the monies he owes on his substantial tax delinquencies.

2. With regard to the statement made concerning gambling, due to the shortness of the hearing, Husband was not able to respond with respect thereto. If there had been sufficient time to do so, he would have strongly disagreed with the amounts claimed that he gambled during the marriage. The fact is that Husband has no money with which to gamble and, as he testified, has not gambled in the last four years. The attempt to introduce pre-divorce conduct as an issue in the modification action several years later should be rejected.

All of the above indicates that for any one of four reasons, the Husband is entitled to a modification in this case:

1. His decrease in income;
2 His decrease in financial status;
3. Her increase in income; and
4. Her increase in financial status.

These changed circumstances clearly demonstrate that Husband is indeed entitled to a temporary modification and he has more than met the burden of showing that there is a "reasonable probability" that he will obtain a revision upon final trial.

Husband is in desperate need of a modification at the earliest possible time, and based upon the uncontradicted evidence in this case, we request that he obtain a temporary modification until the case is heard upon final trial.

Thank you for your kind consideration of the issues in this matter. In the event you are in need of further information, please do not hesitate to contact me.

Respectfully submitted,

Attorney

3. Letter Regarding Defendant's Final Word in Written Closing
Argument for Defendant

Honorable _____
Judge of _____ Court

Re: Plaintiff v. Defendant
 Superior Court of _____ County
 CAFN 12345A

Dear (Judge):

Regarding opposing counsel's letter to you, please let me briefly
respond to certain lettered portions:

A. If the projection set out in the Employer's affidavit is accurate,
then Husband will earn only a total of $5,000 during the last two
months of this year. Needless to say, I believe the facts available January 1 of next year will show that he has earned considerably more than
that.

Furthermore, the mere fact that Husband's percentage participation
in company profits has decreased does not mean he will earn less
income. One assumes that, if the firm has added additional partners,
then the gross income of the firm will increase, which, in turn, would
increase Husband's income.

C. Although Wife's overall financial circumstances may have
increased since the divorce, she essentially has the same assets she had
when Husband left her. The only significant addition has been the
inheritance from her mother's estate.

E. 1. It appears that Husband is taking the position that he should
have an alimony reduction so that he can send one child to medical
school and the other child to graduate school. In effect, he is asking
Wife to pay for the adult children's graduate educations.

Finally, opposing counsel urges that Husband is entitled to a modification because his income and financial status have decreased, and Wife's income and financial status have increased. Without quibbling further over those particular factors, what neither opposing counsel nor his client has addressed is the issue of whether there has been a legitimate decrease in his ability to pay. That is the key issue here, and Husband has not satisfactorily explained why he does not have the ability to pay what he agreed to pay at the time of the divorce in 2001.

Thank you for your continued consideration.

Very truly yours,

Attorney for Defendant

Letter to Judge Explaining Why a Second Temporary Hearing Is Necessary

Honorable _____
Judge of ____Court

Re: Plaintiff v. Defendant
    Superior Court of _____ County
    CAFN 12345A

Dear (Judge):

This letter is in response to the letter to you from opposing counsel that I have just received. While it is true that I had fervently hoped to avoid a second temporary hearing, the facts are that my client is in major financial straits given that he has been paying the mortgage and utilities on the marital residence (where the wife has been residing alone since last July), the minimum monthly payments on the family credit cards, all child care for the child, all living expenses, including an apartment for himself and the child, as well as all fees charged by Drs. _____ & _____. In the meantime, the wife has gotten a job and continues to live in the marital residence by herself, paying none of the expenses and no child support. This state of affairs has been in effect since last summer with no end in sight.

Given that we have no idea when Dr. _____ will complete his child custody report and submit it to the Court, and given further that, once the report is in, counsel will still need some time after reviewing the report to prepare for a final hearing, we are asking for, in effect, emergency relief from the Court at the hearing now scheduled for February 6th as it pertains to financial matters. Now that the wife has a job, there is no reason why she cannot pay child support and move to an apartment so that the husband and child may return to the home. That is the gist of the relief we are seeking on February 6th. 1 am enclosing a copy of our motion, which sets out the problems in greater detail.

As to the access to reports from the professionals, I, too, would like to have copies, but I am familiar with procedure in various Court divisions where copies are not permitted. However, I have an additional problem in that opposing counsel has not agreed for me to review the wife's report from Dr. _____. I believe I have a right to review that report without his permission pursuant to O.C.G.A. § 19-9-4(a) and Davis v. Davis, 253 Ga. 73, 316 S.E.2d 455 (1984) and ask the Court to release that report to me without opposing counsel's consent. Obviously, I have no objection to his reading the report on my client.

Again, our hearing for emergency financial relief scheduled for February 6th is extremely important to my client, and I will plan to be there unless I hear to the contrary from the Court.

Thank you for your attention to this pressing matter.

Respectfully yours,

Attorney for Husband

CHAPTER

11

LETTERS FOR
DIVORCE
LAWYERS

Opposing Counsel
Address

Re: Plaintiff v. Defendant
      Superior Court of _____ County
      CAFN 12345-A

Dear (Attorney):

Enclosed is a draft of a proposed Consent Temporary Order. Please review this and let me know if you see the need for any changes before it is submitted to the Court. I look forward to hearing from you.

Sincerely,

Attorney

Honorable _____
Judge of _____Court

Re: Plaintiff v. Defendant
     Superior Court of _____ County
     CAFN 12345A

Dear (Judge):

Enclosed please find our proposed Order, drafted in accordance with your instructions at the recent hearing in this matter.

This Order was forwarded to opposing counsel on June 1, 2006, and we have today received her permission to sign her name to the same.

Very truly yours,

Attorney

CHAPTER

11

The Honorable _____, Judge
Superior Court of _____ County
Address

    Re: Plaintiff v. Defendant
       Superior Court of _____ County
       CAFN 12345A

Dear (Judge):

    Enclosed please find the original proposed Temporary Order, the format of which has been approved by opposing counsel. If it is acceptable to the Court, I would appreciate it if the Order could be entered and then a copy marked "filed" being returned to me in the enclosed, self-addressed envelope.

                    Very truly yours,

                    Attorney

Client
Address

Re: Plaintiff v. Defendant
   Superior Court of _____ County
   CAFN 12345A

Dear (Client):

   Enclosed are a filed copy of the Consent Temporary Order and a copy of your spouse's discovery request responses. I have not had a chance to review these, so I will depend on you to review them and point out anything that is either unusual or incomplete. Her responses will also show you what type of documents we are required to return to them.
   I hope you had a good vacation, and I assume we are ready to go on the documents. Please let me hear from you.

                                        Very truly yours,

                                        Attorney

CHAPTER

11

LETTERS FOR
DIVORCE
LAWYERS

Client
Address

Re: Plaintiff v. Defendant
    Superior Court of _____ County
    CAFN 12345A

Dear (Client):

Enclosed is a copy of the Consent Temporary Order that has been signed by the Judge and filed with the Clerk. This Order sets out those things that are required of you and your spouse. Please note: if it is not in the Order, it is not a requirement.

I heard from your spouse's attorney earlier today, who advised that the paycheck from the store, which you will receive next week, will have a pay stub attached. That pay stub will be the same each week, and you can also apply those deductions to the net check you received last week.

I hope you feel that things are better now that we are at this point.

                Sincerely,

                Attorney

Letter to Opposing Counsel Approving Temporary Order

Opposing Counsel
Address

Re: Plaintiff v. Defendant
Superior Court of _____ County
CAFN 12345A

Dear (Opposing Counsel):

The separate order concerning access to medical provider documents, etc., in the _____ case that you have drafted is fine. Please
send me a stamped copy when it is entered.

Sincerely,

Attorney

Transmittal Letter to Client with Unfavorable Contempt Order

Client
Address

Re: Plaintiff v. Defendant
    Superior Court of _____ County
    CAFN 12345A

Dear (Client):

Enclosed please find a copy of the Order for Contempt that has been signed by the Judge and entered by the Court. The Judge signed the Order that your spouse's attorney prepared, which included the provision that you pay $3,703.00 to opposing counsel for attorney's and accountant's fees. Also, the Order requires you to "provide full and complete document production and/or explanations for the existence of the following items within seven (7) days of this Order." On pages 4 and 5 of the Order you will see the full list of required items. The Order was filed October 4, so this gives you until the end of next week, October 15, to comply. Based on this experience, I do not believe opposing counsel would hesitate to file another contempt action against you if this Order is not complied with.

Please let me know if you have any questions. I look forward to hearing from you.

Very truly yours,

Attorney

Opposing Counsel
Address

Re: Plaintiff v. Defendant
 Superior Court of _____ County
 CAFN 12345A

Dear (Opposing Counsel):

I write in response to your correspondence dated June 1, 2006, concerning my client's liquidation of assets to pay his temporary alimony and temporary child support obligations pursuant to the Consent Temporary Order entered in this case.

My client very generously agreed to pay $2,500.00 per month in temporary alimony and child support to your client even though his 2006 gross income of $80,000.00 did not justify or even authorize payments aggregating $30,000.00 per year.

In 2005 my client received gross income from his place of employment of only $52,000.00, which would authorize child support of $1,083.00 per month, and not the $1,500.00 per month pursuant to the Temporary Order. As an act of generosity, my client has continued to pay temporary child support and alimony far in excess of his income. It has been my experience that no Judge or jury will ever require a husband to pay more than one-half (1/2) of his net pay. Unfortunately, my client's net pay for 2004 was $41,306.00. His adjusted gross income, which is the correct amount to compute alimony and child support, was only $30,150.00. If my client paid one-half (1/2) of his net pay of $41,306.00, your client would receive $20,653.00. However, much to his credit, my client has continued to pay $30,000.00 per year, which is almost 75 percent of his net pay.

If you and your client desire for us to file a Motion to Modify Downwardly the temporary alimony and child support, please immediately advise me. Otherwise, I will assume that your client agrees that it is appropriate for her spouse to liquidate various assets in order to meet his temporary alimony and child support obligation. Based on reviewing my client's 2004 tax returns, it is obvious to anyone that he must liquidate assets to meet his temporary alimony and child support obligations. It would be literally impossible for a man earning $30,000.00 to pay $30,000.00 per year in temporary alimony and child support.

You also asked that I respond concerning your client's suggestion that all parties meet to reach a mutual agreement resolving this divorce proceeding. In the past, your client has demonstrated a total and completely irrational and unreasonable attitude toward her spouse's ability to pay. He earns from his two jobs with X_____ and Y_____ $52,000.00 in wages. I understand that your client believes he makes many times this amount. However, the reality of the situation is that he earns $52,000.00 per year.

If your client is wiling to approach a settlement agreement in a reasonable and rational fashion, keeping in mind that her spouse earns $52,000.00 per year and acquired all of his wealth prior to ever meeting her, then we would be willing to enter into an open and free dialogue with the hopes of reaching a reasonable resolution of this case. Your client must be reasonable.

Please convey this correspondence to her and contact me concerning the next steps to be taken to resolve this matter.

Sincerely,

Attorney

Client
Address

Re: Plaintiff v. Defendant
    Superior Court of _____ County
        CAFN 12345A

Dear (Client):

Enclosed is a copy of a letter I received from your spouse's attorney in which he admits that your spouse is using assets to pay his current expenses. Mr._____ explains this by saying that his client does not earn enough money from his employment to meet the obligations under the Temporary Order, and he is threatening to petition the Court for a reduction in the amount of his temporary support. He is also saying that your spouse is not willing to talk about the settlement unless the expectations are reduced.

We need to discuss what to do next. We also need to come to an understanding about your attorney's fees, which are building and will continue to build up in this case.

Please give me a call. I look forward to talking with you.

Sincerely,

Attorney

CHAPTER

11

Opposing Counsel
Address

Re: Plaintiff v. Defendant
Superior Court of _____ County
CAFN 12345A

Dear (Opposing Counsel):

I am writing this letter to summarize our agreement today:

1. Your client has agreed to pay an amount equal to the medical insurance deductible for each child and for my client under the Temporary Order. Your client stated that he thought the amount was $300.00 per person. My client is looking for the booklet to verify the deductible amount. I will give her the check for $306.72 from your client for accumulated medical expenses.

2. My client will shop for car insurance to see what coverages she can get and at what costs.

3. Your client will deliver to mine eight (8) floral place mats and the knives and other parts for the Cuisinart. I will give her his check for $79.00 toward a new vacuum cleaner. My client tells me that the photographs of her friends and family are in the dresser located in the dining area near the entrance. She tells me that the two Atlas books are on the bookshelf in the bedroom. Your client will box up these items and give them to my client.

If I have misunderstood or misstated anything, please let me know.

Sincerely,

Attorney

Mediation

Back in the mid-1970s, mediation was almost a four-letter word in the legal community, and attorneys who were flirting around its edges worried about possible malpractice accusations. Now that the courts have discovered it, it seems that mediation is the next best thing to sliced bread. For that reason, if your case is not settled before you file the Divorce Complaint, you may find your case fast-tracked into the mediation process. Even if not required by your Court system, mediation is a worthy alternative to litigation, and you should consider it as a viable option in many cases.

Letter to Client with General Explanation of Mediation

Client
Address

    Re: Plaintiff v. Defendant
        Superior Court of _____ County
        CAFN 12345A

Dear (Client):

As we have discussed, the _____ County Superior Court requires mediation in all divorce cases that are not settled within ninety (90) days of the filing of the Divorce Complaint. Given the current status of your case, I do not believe we will meet the 90-day rule, so we must plan for mediation.

You and I have an appointment to meet with your spouse, her attorney, and a trained mediator at the Courthouse on June 1, 2006, at 10:00 A.M. We are required to bring the following items with us:

1. A completed Financial Affidavit,
2. Completed Interrogatory answers, and
3. The documents listed in the Notice to Produce.

My legal assistant will be in touch with you later this week to arrange for getting these items assembled and prepared. We are required to send copies of these items to your spouse's attorney one week before the mediation. We should also be receiving similar items from your spouse one week before the mediation.

Although each mediator has his or her own style, I have found that mediators generally follow similar procedures for the mediation appointments. Usually, both parties and their attorneys meet with the mediator in a conference room. The mediator will ask each lawyer in turn to describe the overall situation and then describe the specific matters that have been agreed to and the matters where there is no agreement. For instance, you and your spouse have already agreed to joint custody of the children, but you have not agreed on time-sharing or on how child support should be handled.

After the mediator has defined the issues where there is no agreement, the mediator will review the Financial Affidavits, Interrogatories and other documents. Once that is completed, the mediator will tackle each matter, identify the issues of contention, and then try to work through them with you and your spouse. Both attorneys will be present. If the tension level is too high, the mediator may call a caucus and separate the parties—you and I will go to one room and your spouse and her lawyer will go to another—and the mediator goes back and forth. It is sort of a "shuttle diplomacy" process.

Sometimes it is possible to settle everything, at which point the mediator will prepare a memorandum of understanding for all parties to sign. This memorandum is then used to prepare a formal Settlement Agreement by one of the attorneys.

Sometimes there is enough progress so that the mediator believes it worthwhile to schedule another meeting. Sometimes absolutely nothing happens and the mediator declares a stalemate. If that happens, we will start preparing for trial. Even if we are unable to work out a complete settlement during mediation, we may be able to narrow the issues, and we should also have a better idea of your spouse's positions on different points. I believe mediation is a worthwhile process and may be beneficial.

I do not expect this letter to answer all of your questions, but I did want to give you an overview of this part of the divorce process before we get into it. Please do not hesitate to ask questions.

Sincerely,

Attorney

Letter to Opposing Counsel to Lay Groundwork for Mediation

Opposing Counsel
Address

Re: Plaintiff v. Defendant
    Superior Court of _____ County
    CAFN 12345A

Dear (Opposing Counsel):

    After discussing all of the issues with my client, _____, I believe it would be worthwhile to attempt mediation in this case. It appears that my client and his spouse still enjoy a civil relationship and have worked out an agreeable co-parenting schedule for the children. If your client is amenable to the idea, I propose _____X, _____Y, or _____Z as potential mediators. We may use my office or come to yours, as you and your client prefer.

    Please let me know if mediation is a viable option and if any of the proposed mediators are acceptable. If so, I will be happy to handle the logistics.

                      Sincerely,

                      Attorney

Letter to Client About Scheduling Mediation

Client
Address

   Re: Plaintiff v. Defendant
   Superior Court of _____ County
   CAFN 12345A

Dear (Client):

   As you can see from the enclosed, I have proposed the idea of mediation to your spouse's attorney. However, we have just over two weeks before the 30-Day Conference, so I suggest you go ahead with document collection and answers to the Interrogatories. As soon as I have had a response to my letter, I will be in touch, but in the meantime, if you have questions or comments, please give me a call.

                    Sincerely,

                    Attorney

Letter to Opposing Counsel with Proposed
Consent Order for Mediation

Opposing Counsel
Address

Re: Plaintiff v. Defendant
Superior Court of _____ County
CAFN 12345A

Dear (Opposing Counsel):

Enclosed is a proposed Consent Order taking this case off Judge _____'s calendar so that we can try mediation. If this Order meets with your approval, please sign and file it with the Court. I would appreciate a stamped copy. As we discussed, I will call (Mediator) and see what times are available to schedule a mediation session. I will be in touch as soon as I have some information.

Sincerely,

Attorney

Mediator
Address

    Re: Plaintiff v. Defendant
       Superior Court of _____ County
       CAFN 12345A

Dear (Mediator):

This letter is to confirm that we have scheduled mediation with you in the above-referenced case for 9:00 A.M. on Thursday, June 1, 2006, at your office. Unless you hear shortly from the Plaintiff's counsel, _____, that her client will be out of town that day, I will look forward to seeing you on June 1, 2006.

               Very truly yours,

               Attorney

CHAPTER

LETTERS FOR
DIVORCE
LAWYERS

Letter to Court Mediation Supervisor

ADR Director
Alternative Dispute Resolution Office
Address

Re: Plaintiff v. Defendant
   Superior Court of _____ County
   CAFN 12345A

Dear (ADR Director):

   Enclosed please find the Mediation Initiation Form and copies of the Complaint, Answer, and Counterclaim. I am forwarding a copy of the Mediation Form and Instructions to opposing counsel. I am hopeful that she and I can select a mediator and set up the mediation without further assistance from your office. I will be in touch if necessary.

                              Sincerely,

                              Attorney

Trial

D espite your best efforts and fervent wishes, your case has not settled, and it is going to trial. It is time to do your planning, prepare your client, and gather up your witnesses.

Client
Address

Re: Plaintiff v. Defendant (insert style of case)
Superior Court of _____ County
CAFN 12345A

Dear (Client):

In preparation for trial, your spouse's attorney has served subpoenas on the following: _____ Drugs; _____'s Hair Salon; _____'s Grocery; _____ Pharmacy; and _____ Jewelry Store. I imagine these witnesses are being called to testify about your spending habits, but in order to make sure, please get in touch with each one and ask that they give me a call as soon as possible.

Sincerely,

Attorney

Letter to Client with Affidavit Form

(Note: Make sure these are permissible and admissible in your jurisdiction before using.)

Client
Address

Re: Plaintiff v. Defendant (insert style of case)
Superior Court of _____ County
CAFN 12345A

Dear (Client):

As you and I discussed, the Judge will look at affidavits from people who know you and your parenting abilities and skills. I think we should have as many as we can gather. The text of the affidavit should be realistic and not paint you as parent of the year. It is more believable if it includes some weaknesses as well as strengths. (If it leans too heavily on the weakness side, we do not have to use it.) Enclosed is an affidavit form consisting of three pages. You may make as many copies of this as you need.

In order to use this, the Affiant (person signing the affidavit) should fill in his or her name on the first page. The blank page, page number two, can be used for a handwritten or typed statement by the Affiant. If the person needs additional sheets, go ahead and add them. The Affiant should identify himself/herself and explain his/her connection to you; i.e., your brother, next-door neighbor for five years, your pastor, your boss—whatever. Then the Affiant should give observations and conclusions about you and your child.

Finally, when the statement is complete, the affidavit should be stapled together. Then the Affiant must date and sign the affidavit in front of a notary public who then must notarize the affidavit. If you have any questions about how to make use of this, please let me know.

Sincerely,

Attorney

CHAPTER

13

LETTERS FOR
DIVORCE
LAWYERS

Loan Officer for _____, Inc.
_____ Bank
Account Services — 00000
Address
Attention: _____

Re: Subpoena for Trial of Plaintiff v. Defendant
    CAFN 12345A
    Superior Court of _____ County

Dear (Loan Officer):

I represent the Plaintiff, _____, in the above-referenced case, which is currently pending in the Superior Court of _____ County. Enclosed is a subpoena requiring your attendance at 1:30 P.M. on Tuesday, June 6, 2006, for the trial of that case. Also enclosed is my firm's check for $28.00 for one day's attendance at the trial.

Because of the uncertainty about the actual time for commencement of the trial, you do not need to actually appear at the Court on Tuesday, June 6, 2006, <u>as long as</u> you provide me with a telephone number and address where you can be reached <u>immediately and at all times</u> during business hours <u>and</u> as long as you can appear in Court within one hour of notification to appear. Please call me or my associate, _____, in this office immediately to confirm that you have received this subpoena and to give us your contact information. If neither of us is available, please leave a comprehensive voicemail message.

Please note that this case is on a one-week trial calendar and may be reached for trial at any point during the week of Monday, June 5, 2006, through Friday, June 9, 2006. Because there are two cases ahead of this case, neither the Court nor I know when, or even if, this case will actually begin during that one-week period. If this case cannot be reached this week, it will be rescheduled to a later trial calendar. You are under subpoena until the trial of this case is concluded, whether it is tried this week or at some time in the future. If it is not reached during this term, I will contact you as soon as I know the dates of the next trial term.

When the trial of this case actually begins, you will be notified, and we will try to give you an estimate of when you will be needed in Court. We will do all that we reasonably can do to minimize the inconvenience to you.

If you have questions regarding this letter or the subpoena, please give me a call. As mentioned before, you must call me in any event to leave your telephone numbers and addresses.

Very truly yours,

Attorney

Settlements

The settlement process can occur in one (or more) of several ways. Unless the settlement is being promoted through mediation, proposals are going back and forth in letter form or embodied within a written Agreement format. In this situation, it is essential that the client sees each and every version before it goes to opposing counsel. Although the letter format is shorter and easier to read and comprehend, it is probably a good idea to convert to settlement Agreement format early on, so everyone has a chance to review the boilerplate before the deal is finalized. If you prefer to be the Agreement scrivener, then put the initial offer or a later counteroffer into an Agreement format. By doing this, you can usually be assured that your Agreement format and boilerplate will be that which is used.

Settlement Offer to Opposing Counsel

Opposing Counsel
Address

Re: Plaintiff v. Defendant
    Superior Court of _____ County
    CAFN 12345A

Dear (Opposing Counsel):

The intention of this letter is to offer a negotiated settlement of the outstanding issues of custody and related matters in this case. The purpose of this letter is to finalize all issues and create an environment in which both parties can work together effectively as co-parents of their child, _____.

This offer will remain open for acceptance by a written response received in my office prior to noon, June 1, 2006. If not accepted by this time, this offer will lapse and become void.

As related to the already signed co-parenting plan dated May 1, 2006, the following sets out the items that remain undecided as indicated by italicized and bold print within the body of the signed plan. Following is my client's offer as it relates to the unagreed items in the May 1, 2006, co-parenting plan:

1. Mother and father share joint physical and legal custody (p. 2).
2. Father maintains primary residence for school district purposes (pgs. 2, 10).
3. Mother has the final say if the parties cannot agree on medical/dental/psychological issues (pgs. 2, 10, 16).
4. Mother has the final say if the parties cannot agree on religious issues provided that mother's decisions shall not interfere with father's regularly scheduled time with child (pgs. 2, 10, 16).
5. Father retains final decisions on education/daycare and activities if the parties are unable to agree (pgs. 2, 10).
6. Each parent shall provide total transportation for child when child is with that parent (p. 5).
7. All expenses detailed in the co-parenting plan will be shared on a 60 percent father, 40 percent mother ratio (p. 5) .

8. If the child's transfers from parent to parent do not occur at daycare or school, then the transfers shall alternate between _____ Park and _____ Park (p. 5).
9. Both parents agree to honor a first-right-of-refusal for childcare over eight (8) hours (p. 11).
10. Father shall provide medical insurance coverage for the child as long as said coverage is available for the child as an employee benefit from the father's employer or the mother's employer. If the mother's employer provides the insurance coverage, the father shall be responsible only for that portion of the premium that provides coverage for the child. If neither party has medical insurance coverage available for the child as an employee benefit, then the parties shall purchase comparable insurance and father shall pay 60 percent and the mother shall pay 40 percent of the required premium (p. 15).
11. Neither party shall expose the child to guns or ammunition either directly or indirectly, until she is at least sixteen (16) years of age (p. 17).
12. Mother shall schedule the child's medical and dental appointments after consulting with father for convenient appointment times (p. 18).

In addition to the items from the co-parenting plan, my client offers the following:

- Father shall be solely responsible for the psychological testing expenses incurred in this matter and waives the right to collect $2,000.00 from mother.
- Father waives any right to reimbursement for telephone expenses.
- Mother waives any claims to insurance reimbursement funds or child support expenses incurred prior to this date.
- Each party pays his or her own attorneys' fees and expenses.
- The final decree will be entered prior to January 1, 2006.

If these terms are acceptable, please let me know and I will prepare an Agreement to cover these issues. I will also prepare a decree that incorporates this second Agreement and the co-parenting plan. The first Agreement is already incorporated into a permanent Order.

This offer is made for compromise and settlement of the issues in this case and shall be used for no other purpose. Specifically, the contents of this letter shall neither be tendered nor admitted as evidence in any hearing or trial in this matter except as same relates to the issue of attorneys' fees.

I hope that we can settle this case in this manner and preserve the improved working and co-parenting relationship that our clients have been able to achieve through the co-parenting program over the past nine months.

I look forward to hearing from you on this matter.

Sincerely,

Attorney

Opposing Counsel
Address

    Re: Plaintiff v. Defendant
        Superior Court of _____ County
        CAFN 12345A

Dear (Opposing Counsel):

    As you are aware, my client would like very much to reach a permanent settlement in this matter so that she and your client can get on with their respective lives. We have reviewed the situation, and she has authorized me to make the following proposal of settlement:

1. <u>Custody</u>: The parties shall have joint legal custody of the children and they shall have joint and equal responsibility regarding major decisions to be made in the rearing of the children. However, in the event they are unable to reach agreement as to a major decision concerning the children, then the mother's decision shall control. The mother shall have permanent physical custody of the children.

2. <u>Visitation</u>: The father shall have the right to visit with the children any time and at all times the parties agree. In the event the parties are unable to agree, then the father shall have, as a minimum, the following visitation:

    (a) The first and third weekends of each month from Friday at 6:00 P.M. until Sunday at 6:00 P.M., with the first weekend being that weekend that includes the first Friday. If a visitation weekend is followed by a national holiday, then the visitation shall end on that Monday at 6:00 P.M.

    (b) On the second and fourth non-holiday Monday of each month from 6:00 P.M. until 8:00 P.M.

    (c) Every Wednesday from 6:00 P.M. until he returns them to school the following morning. If there is no school that Thursday, then the father will return the children to the mother at 3:30 P.M.

(d) One-half of the winter vacation each year. The father will have the children the first half of the vacation in the odd-numbered years and the second half of the vacation in the even-numbered years.

(e) Thanksgiving from 6:00 P.M. on the day school closes until 6:00 P.M. on the Sunday following Thanksgiving in every even-numbered year. The mother will have the children for this period in every odd-numbered year.

(f) Rosh Hashanah—from 6:00 P.M. on the day preceding Rosh Hashanah until 6:00 P.M. on the first day in the even-numbered years and from 6:00 P.M. on the first day until 6:00 P.M. on the second day in the odd-numbered years. The children will be with the mother the alternate time.

(g) Passover—from 6:00 P.M. on the day preceding Passover until 6:00 P.M. on the first day in the odd-numbered years and from 6:00 P.M. on the first day until 6:00 P.M. on the second day in the even-numbered years, with the mother having the children in the alternate years.

(h) Summer vacation—For a minimum of two weeks in the summer. The first week will begin on the third Friday of June at 6:00 P.M. and continue until 6:00 P.M. on the following Friday. The second week will begin on the first Friday in August and continue until 6:00 P.M. on the following Friday. The mother will have the children with her without interruption for the second week of July and the second week of August.

(i) Summer travel—The mother will have the right to take the children to Israel every other year for six weeks during the summer vacation to visit family. The father will have the right to have the children with him during a portion of that time in Israel, if he wishes to make the trip also. In the event he does wish to make a trip to Israel during the time the mother and the children are there, he and the mother will finalize their plans for the children by April 15.

3. Child Support: Your client, the father, will provide the following for the support of the children:

(a) $3,500 per month until both children have reached the age of 18 years, unless the children have not yet finished high school, in which event the child support will continue until both children have graduated from high school or reached the age of 21 years.

(b) All medical, dental, psychological, and orthodontic expenses for the children as long as your client is also paying child support.

(c) Tuition so the children may continue in private school.

(d) The expenses necessary for each child to receive a four-year college degree.

(e) Life insurance on his life in the amount of $500,000 as long as your client continues to have other obligations under the terms of the Agreement. In the event of your client's death, the insurance proceeds will be paid to my client as the children's trustee.

4. Spousal Support: Your client will provide the following for my client:

(a) Medical and dental insurance coverage as available under COBRA.

(b) Her attorney's fees and the litigation expenses that have been incurred in this matter.

5. Property Settlement:

(a) Your client will transfer to mine the real property located at 000 _____ Street, _____, Georgia, free of all encumbrances.

(b) The younger child's baby bed, and the children's baby clothing, baby toys and equipment

(c) Those items included in paragraph 24 of the Temporary Order, most of which my client has already received.

6. Gett: Your client will participate as necessary and pay one-half (1/2) of the expenses required to obtain a Gett within 45 days following the granting of the civil divorce.

I believe this proposal has much merit; it is simple, uncomplicated, and does not interfere with your client's ongoing businesses.

This offer is made for the purpose of compromise and settlement of the issues in this case and shall be used for no other purpose. Specifically, the contents of this letter shall neither be tendered nor admitted into evidence for any reason in this matter except as same may be relevant to the issues of attorney's fees. This offer shall remain open for written acceptance until 5:00 P.M. on June 1, 2006. If not accepted by that time, this offer shall be rescinded and become void at that time.

Please discuss this offer with your client at your earliest convenience, and let me know if we might structure a settlement Agreement along these lines. I look forward to hearing from you.

Sincerely,

Attorney

Letter to Opposing Counsel Proposing Partial Settlement—Financial Issues Only

Opposing Counsel
Address

Re: Plaintiff v. Defendant
    Superior Court of _____ County
    CAFN 12345A

Dear (Opposing Counsel):

For a number of reasons, my client will be moving from his present apartment by June 1, and he would like to try to settle the property and debt issues before he moves.

A review of the overall situation as to debt and property shows the following:

1. Marital property:

    A   Residence—Fair Market Value $200,000.00;
    B   A portion of my client's 401(k), which was accumulated during the marriage; and
    C   A few pieces of furniture.

2. Marital debt:

    A. Mortgage on the home—$209,000.00;
    B. MasterCard—$2,650.00;
    C. Visa—$5,300.00;
    D. Visa—$10,600.00;
    E. MasterCard $4,000.00; and
    F. Visa—$12,700.00.

* The B. MasterCard debt and the F. Visa debt were created from transferring balances from your client's Visa account of $10,400.00 and her second Visa of $3,300.00, to a lower-interest-rate card, which happened to be in my client's name. These two debts of approximately $13,700.00 were hers at the time of the marriage. He, of course, has documents to substantiate this.

When they bought the home in June 1998, it appraised for $180,000. The original mortgage was $160,500.00 and the second mortgage (for bill consolidation) was $44,500.00. The second mortgage funds were used for the following purposes:

1. Pay off her car loan $2,800.00;
2. Pay off his car lease $9,900.00;
3. Pay off his credit cards, including $5,500.00 of charges made by her—$16,500.00;
4. Interior painting and carpet—$6,200.00;
5. Other home improvements—$2,000.00;
5. Moving expenses—$2,000.00; and
6 Origination fee—$4,600.00.

They refinanced the home in June 2002 in order to go from a 30-year mortgage to a 15-year mortgage, the idea being that the house would be paid for before their child began college. In addition, the second mortgage at 15.25 percent was replaced by a new mortgage at 8 percent. When the refinancing took place, the funds were disbursed as follows:

1. Pay off original mortgage $165,485.04
2. Pay off second mortgage   47,223.70
3. Closing costs   + 365.18
                                $ 216,390.92
4. Loan amount   - 211,500.00
5. Paid by him at closing   5,101.60

The bottom line is that the house is mortgaged to the hilt; there is additional marital credit card debt of $35,000.00 and no other property to speak of with any value. With these facts in mind, my client makes the following offer to settle the property and debt issues:

1. He will assume sole and total responsibility for all debt listed above;
2. He will receive sole title to and possession of the home no later than June 15, 2006;
3. He will keep his retirement account;
4. He will keep his automobile;
5. He will keep all of the personal property, furniture, furnishings, appliances, etc., that he had before the marriage;
6. She will keep her car;
7. She will keep all of her retirement funds;

8. She will keep all of the personal property, furniture, furnishings, etc., which she had before the marriage;

9. She will be relieved of all obligations for the mortgage and listed credit card debt;

10. The parties will divide the wedding gifts and other personal property acquired during the marriage.

The net result to her is that she will have everything she had before the marriage except $13,700.00 of credit card debt. If we are not able to settle these issues, then both parties will have to deal with a home with a negative value and the credit card debt. Even though she has done relatively well financially in this case so far, I believe it is quite unrealistic for her to believe that she will receive the home and that he will pay for the home and all of the debt.

This offer is made for the sole purpose of settlement and compromise of the issues in this matter and may be used for no other purpose. Specifically, the contents of this letter may neither be tendered nor admitted at any hearing or trial in this matter except as same may be relative to the issue of attorney's fees. This offer shall remain open for written acceptance until 5:00 P.M. on May 15, 2006. If not accepted by that time, this offer shall be rescinded, and my client will make other arrangements for housing.

I hope your client will consider this as a way to rid herself of all the marital debt and get a clean start financially. Please discuss this offer with her, and let me hear if we might settle the property and debt issues along these lines. I look forward to hearing from you.

Sincerely,

Attorney

14

Letter to Opposing Counsel Disputing Terms
of Proposed Temporary Order

Opposing Counsel

Address

Re: Plaintiff v. Defendant
Superior Court of _____ County
CAFN 12345A

Dear (Opposing Counsel):

I have received your letter of June 1, 2006, and I have reviewed it for consistency with what the transcript indicates the Judge said in Court. In response, let me point out the following:

1. CUSTODY: As I interpret the CUSTODY paragraph, the Judge awarded joint custody to the parties. Then, on page 2, he reminded the parties and specifically my client, the mother, that "the question of custody of the child is always for the Court to decide. The jury never decides that." As I read your proposed order, it presumes an automatic change of custody if there is any alleged use of alcohol by my client. As long as this order clearly states that any change will take place only after proper notice, a hearing, and a decision by the Judge, then I have no problem. Of course, custody of the child would be denied to either parent, I assume, if there were any use of alcohol by that parent.

2. MARITAL HOME: If you will review my proposed order, in the second sentence of the second paragraph I wrote, "Plaintiff shall sign any documents necessary to carry out the refinancing of the home." I believe that is what the Judge said.

3. ALCOHOL USE: Again, the Judge did not order an automatic change of custody, which your language implies. Certainly, if your client believes there is any problem with my client's care of the child, he has the right to bring it to the Court's attention, but the Judge did not order an automatic custody change without a hearing.

4. SUPPORT PAYMENTS: Regarding support payments, I find absolutely nothing in the transcript to indicate that the Judge left this decision to your client. The judge simply said, "$4,200 a month will be the

payment. And whether it's child support or alimony for two months, I don't know that it's going to make a whole lot of difference." Your client then complained about the dollar amount, but there was <u>no</u> discussion that he would have the right to decide how to apportion it between child support and alimony. I am certain your client wants it to be all alimony and, of course, my client wants it to be all child support. We may need to leave this up to the Judge.

5.   UTILITIES: Again, if you will refer to my proposed order in the third paragraph of MARITAL HOME, you will see that it says, "Plaintiff shall pay the ordinary household expenses and utilities incurred in connection with the residence after June 1, 2006." Since that language is included, I am not sure what the problem is.

In reviewing your revised order, I have the following issues:

6.   CUSTODY: You have used the phrase, "conditioned on the Plaintiff receiving formal counseling for her drinking and abstaining from the use of alcohol, as hereinafter set forth." As I mentioned above, in the event there is any particular behavior, including use of alcohol, which appears to be a problem, then it can be brought to the Court's attention. However, there is no automatic change of custody triggered without a Court hearing, and this should be clearly stated in the order.

7.   VISITATION: Your language is acceptable, although I do not think my client has any plans for a vacation.

8.   MARITAL HOME: I believe we have said the same things but in different places. I put all provisions relating to the home under MARITAL HOME, including possession, temporary use of furniture, payments for the home, as well as the utilities and repairs. For the layperson it is easier to follow an order if all provisions relating to a particular subject are grouped together.

9.   ALIMONY: I have already discussed this topic above. Because of the tax consequences, we have elected that the amount be child support. Secondly, I have included the information about household expenses and utilities under the MARITAL HOME provision, but its location is not particularly important.

10. IT IS FURTHER ORDERED . . . : There is nothing in the transcript that is remotely similar to this provision and it should be deleted.

Please let me know if we agree on these matters. If not, then we will have to present separate proposed Orders to the Judge.

On a separate matter, I received your voicemail message about your client's documents that are still at the marital home. Please let me know when he wants to retrieve them, and I will ask my client to let him remove all documents and personal papers from the home.

I look forward to hearing from you.

Sincerely,

Attorney

Client
Address

     Re: Plaintiff v. Defendant
        Superior Court of _____ County
        CAFN 12345A

Dear (Client):

    Enclosed is a rough draft of a Settlement Agreement that I have prepared from my notes made during our conference yesterday. I have left in a provision for alimony but without an amount. I recommend that we not actually ask for alimony, however. After you have read through this, please give me a call so we can discuss possible changes before I send it to opposing counsel.

    I look forward to hearing from you.

                   Sincerely,

                   Attorney

Transmittal Letter to Client with Draft of Agreement

Client
Address

Re: Plaintiff v. Defendant
Superior Court of _____ County
CAFN 12345A

Dear (Client):

Enclosed is a rough draft of a revised Agreement. I believe I have picked up the important parts, left out the superfluous parts, and kept the legalese/boilerplate to a minimum. Please review this and let me know if we need to make further changes before this document is presented to opposing counsel.

Sincerely,

Attorney

Example of a Settlement Agreement of Unmarried Parents with One Child—Bare Minimum

IN THE SUPERIOR COURT OF _____ COUNTY
STATE OF GEORGIA

_____,)
)

Plaintiff, _____

)

vs.   )   CIVIL ACTION FILE
)   NO. 0000000000

_____.)
)

Defendant,

SETTLEMENT AGREEMENT

This Agreement, made and entered into by and between _____ (hereinafter referred to as "Mother") and _____ (hereinafter referred to as "Father"):

WITNESSETH

WHEREAS, the parties are the natural parents of _____, who was born April 20, 2004, age 2; and

WHEREAS, the parties wish to resolve all issues concerning custody, child support, and visitation; and

WHEREAS, the parties have defined the respective rights and obligations regarding these issues, and all other matters;

NOW THEREFORE, for and in consideration of their mutual promises to each other, and the benefits flowing to each party, they do hereby mutually covenant and agree as follows:

ITEM 1. CUSTODY

The Mother shall have sole legal and physical custody of the minor child of the parties, (child's name).

ITEM 2. VISITATION

The Father shall have the right to visit with the child at such times and for such periods of time as are agreed upon by the parties.

ITEM 3. CHILD SUPPORT

The Father or his estate shall pay to the Mother the sum of One Thousand Six Hundred Sixteen Dollars and 67/100 ($1,616.67) per month for the support, maintenance and education of (child's name), said payments to continue until the child reaches the age of eighteen (18) years, dies, marries, or becomes self-supporting, whichever event shall first occur; provided, however, that if the child is still attending high school as a regular full-time student when he attains the age of eighteen (18) years, the child support shall continue until the child has graduated from or terminates his high school education or reaches the age of twenty (20) years, whichever shall first occur.

Said payment shall be paid on the first day of each month, beginning May 1, 2006, and shall continue to be paid on the first day of each month thereafter as hereinabove provided. All payments due hereunder shall be paid by the Father's employer pursuant to an Income Deduction Order.

In January of each year during which child support is due, beginning January 2007, the Father shall modify the then current child support payment amount so that the new amount is reflective of twenty percent (20%) of the Father's gross income from all sources for the previous calendar tax year. The Father shall provide to the Mother copies of all forms W-2 and 1099 received by him reflecting income received during the past calendar tax year. In addition, on or before April 15 of each year, the Father shall provide to the Mother a signed copy of his federal income tax return, as filed and when filed, for the previous year.

The child support payable herein is for one minor child and the applicable percentage of the Father's gross income is 17-23 percent. The gross income of the Father is approximately $97,000.00 per annum and the gross income of the Mother is approximately $18,000.00 per annum. There are no special factors to consider in setting the amount of child support.

Wherever, in violation of the terms of this Agreement, there shall have been a failure to make the support payments due hereunder so that the amount unpaid is equal to or greater than the amount payable for one month, then the payments required to be made may be collected by the process of continuing garnishment for support.

ITEM 4. ADDITIONAL CHILD SUPPORT

As additional support for the minor child of the parties, the Father or his estate shall reimburse the Mother for certain out-of-pocket expenses previously incurred by her in the total amount of Five Thousand Four Hundred Dollars ($5,400.00). The Father shall pay said amount to the Mother at the rate of $225.00 per month, beginning May 1, 2006, and continuing thereafter for twenty-four (24) months or until a total of Five Thousand Four Hundred Dollars ($5,400.00) has been fully paid, whichever first occurs.

ITEM 5. CHARGE AGAINST ESTATE

All payments due hereunder shall be paid by the Father, or his estate, to the Mother. In the event the Father should die prior to the fulfillment of all payment obligations set out in this Agreement, then the Father's estate shall be obligated to complete all payments set out elsewhere in this Agreement. This obligation shall be a first lien against the Father's estate, provisions of the Father's Last Will and Testament to the contrary notwithstanding.

ITEM 6. DISCOVERY WAIVER

Each party acknowledges that procedures are available under the Georgia Civil Practice Act to fully inquire into and investigate the assets, income, and liabilities of the other party before considering any settlement in this matter. Each party further acknowledges that those procedures have not been fully utilized and that this Agreement has been negotiated and reached without the benefit of full discovery. Each party hereby specifically waives her or his rights to additional discovery and accepts the terms set out in this Agreement in full satisfaction of all rights and claims against the other party.

ITEM 7. BINDING EFFECT

Except as otherwise provided herein, this Settlement Agreement shall be fully binding on the parties and their heirs, legatees, executors, administrators, and assigns.

ITEM 8. SEVERABILITY OF TERMS

In the event any paragraph or paragraphs of this Settlement Agreement shall be declared invalid or void by any Court, such declaration shall not invalidate the entire Agreement, and all other paragraphs of this Settlement Agreement shall remain in full force and effect. It is the intent of the parties that any provision or clause of this Agreement that is held invalid under the laws of this State shall be ineffective to the extent that it is prohibited but it shall not affect the validity of the entire Agreement.

ITEM 9. ENTIRETY OF AGREEMENT

This Agreement constitutes the entire understanding of the parties, and there are no representations or warranties other than those expressly set forth herein.

Except as specifically provided herein, no modification or waiver of any of the terms hereof shall be valid unless in writing and signed by both parties. No waiver of any breach hereof or default hereunder shall be deemed a waiver of any subsequent breach or default of a similar nature.

This Agreement shall be construed and governed in accordance with the laws of the State of Georgia.

ITEM 10. UNDERSTANDING AND ASSENT

The parties acknowledge that they each are entering into this Agreement freely and voluntarily; that they each have made a full disclosure of all facts that may be relevant to this Agreement to the other; that they each have arrived at the terms of this Agreement through the process of negotiation through counsel; that they each have ascertained and weighed all of the facts and circumstances likely to influence their legal decisions independently of the other; that they have each been provided the opportunity to review this Agreement with counsel independently of the other; that they have each given due consideration to the provisions contained within this Agreement; and that they each clearly understand and assent to all of the provisions hereof.

IN WITNESS WHEREOF, the parties have signed their names and affixed their seals to three counterparts of this Agreement, each of which shall be enforceable as an original, this day _____ of April 2006.

_____

_____, Plaintiff

Subscribed before me this
_____ Day of April, 2006.

_____

Notary Public

_____

_____, Defendant

Subscribed before me this
_____ Day of April, 2006.

_____

Notary Public

IN THE SUPERIOR COURT OF _____ COUNTY
STATE OF GEORGIA

_____,)

)

Plaintiff,   )

)

vs.   )   CIVIL ACTION
)   FILE NO. 0000000000000

_____( )

)

Defendant,

SEPARATION AGREEMENT

This Agreement made and entered into by and between (name of Wife) (hereinafter referred to as "Wife"), and (name of Husband) (hereinafter referred to as "Husband"):
WITNESSETH:

WHEREAS, Husband and Wife were married on _____ , 1996; and

WHEREAS, two children were born as issue of the marriage, being (name of Child); born _____, 1999, age 7; and (name of Child), born _____, 2002, age 4; and

WHEREAS, neither party to this Agreement is laboring under any disabilities at law; and

WHEREAS, unfortunate differences have arisen between the parties as a result of which Husband and Wife have agreed to separate and live apart from each other in a bona fide state of separation; and

WHEREAS, Husband and Wife wish to settle all issues as to custody, visitation, child support, alimony, division of property, payment of debts, and any and all claims and rights of any nature whatsoever either may have against the other;

NOW, THEREFORE, in consideration of the covenants, promises, Agreements and other valuable consideration that is hereinafter set forth, the parties agree as follows:

ITEM 1. NO INTERFERENCE

Each party shall be free from the interference, authority, and control, direct or indirect, by the other, as fully as if she or he were single and unmarried; neither party shall harass, molest, or interfere with the other or compel or endeavor to compel the other to cohabit or dwell with him or her,

ITEM 2. CUSTODY

The Wife shall have permanent legal and physical custody of the minor children of the parties:

being _____, born _____, 1999, age 7; and _____, born _____, 2002, age 4;

ITEM 3. VISITATION

The Husband shall have the right to visit with the children apart from the residence of Wife as follows:

(a) every other weekend from Friday from 8:00 P.M. until the following Sunday at 6:30 P.M.;

(b) for the Wednesday before Thanksgiving in every even-numbered year, from 5:30 P.M. until 10:00 P.M.; provided that the Wife shall have the children with her for this same period of time in every odd-numbered year, the Husband's other visitation rights notwithstanding;

(c) for Thanksgiving Day in every odd-numbered year from 10:00 A.M. until 10:00 P.M.; provided that the Wife shall have the children with her for this same period of time in every even-numbered year, the Husband's other visitation rights notwithstanding;

(d) for the first night of Chanukah in every even-numbered year from 6:00 P.M. until 8:00 P.M.; provided that the Wife shall have the children with her for this same period of time in every odd-numbered year, the Husband's other visitation rights notwithstanding;

(e) for the second night of Chanukah in every odd-numbered year from 6:00 P.M. until 8:00 P.M.; provided that the Wife shall have the children with her for this same period of time in every odd-numbered year, the Husband's other visitation rights notwithstanding;

(f) for two consecutive weeks between June 15 and August 15 each year, provided the Husband has given written notice of his visitation plans to the Wife prior to May 1 each year;

(g) from 7:00 P.M. on December 31 in each even-numbered year until 7:00 P.M. the following day; provided the Wife shall have the children with her for this same period of time in every odd-numbered year, the Husband's other visitation rights notwithstanding;

(h) on New Year's Day in every even-numbered year from 10:00 A.M. until 9:00 P.M.; provided the Wife shall have the children with her for this same period of time in every odd-numbered year, the Husband's other visitation rights notwithstanding;

(i) if the Martin Luther King, Jr. holiday follows a weekend during which the children are otherwise with the Husband, then said visitation shall be extended until 7:30 P.M. of the holiday in every even-numbered year; provided the Wife shall have the children with her for this same period of time in every odd-numbered year, the Husband's other visitation rights notwithstanding;

(j) from 5:00 P.M. until 7:00 P.M. on February 14 each year;

(k) for the first Seder of Passover from 5:30 P.M. until 9:00 P.M. in every odd-numbered year; provided the Wife shall have the children with her for this same period of time in every odd-numbered year, the Husband's other visitation rights notwithstanding;

(l) for the second Seder of Passover from 5:30 P.M. until 9:00 P.M. in every even-numbered year; provided the Wife shall have the children with her for this same period of time in every odd-numbered year, the Husband's other visitation rights notwithstanding;

(m) for the first twenty-four-hour period of each child's Spring break each year;

(n) for the Purim Carnival at the Synagogue in every odd-numbered year from 8:30 A.M. until 7:30 P.M.;

(o) if the Memorial Day holiday follows a weekend during which the children are otherwise with the Husband, then said visitation shall be extended until 7:30 P.M. of the holiday in even-numbered years; provided the Wife shall have the children with her for this same period of time in every odd-numbered year, the Husband's other visitation rights notwithstanding;

(p) from 7:30 P.M. until 9:00 P.M. on June 9 each year; provided that the children shall be with the Wife on June 22 each year, the Husband's other visitation rights notwithstanding

(q) for Father's Day each year from 10:00 A.M. until 10:00 P.M.; provided that the children shall spend that same period of time on Mother's Day each year with the Wife, the Husband's other visitation rights notwithstanding;

(r) from 7:30 P.M. on July 3 until 10:00 P.M. on July 4 in each even-numbered year; provided the children are not in summer camp and provided further that the children shall spend this same period of time with the Wife in every odd-numbered year, the Husband's other visitation rights notwithstanding;

(s) if the Labor Day holiday follows a weekend during which the children are otherwise with the Husband, then said visitation shall be extended until 7:30 P.M. of the holiday in every odd-numbered year; provided the Wife shall have the children with her for this same period of time in every even-numbered year, the Husband's other visitation rights notwithstanding;

(t) on _____ each year from 7:30 P.M. until 9:30 P.M. for the older child's birthday; provided that the children shall spend the following day with the Wife each year, the Husband's other visitation rights notwithstanding;

(u) for the first day of Rosh Hashanah in every even-numbered year from 5:30 P.M. the evening before until 7:30 P.M. on the first day; provided that the Wife shall have the Children with her for this same period of time in every odd-numbered year, the Husband's other visitation rights notwithstanding;

(v) for the second day of Rosh Hashanah in every odd-numbered year from 5:30 P.M. the evening before until 7:30 P.M. on the first day; provided that the Wife shall have the children with her for this same period of time in every even-numbered year, the Husband's other visitation rights notwithstanding;

(w) for the Eve of Yom Kippur in every even-numbered year from 5:30 P.M. until 10:30 P.M.; provided that the Wife shall have the Children with her for this same period of time in every odd-numbered year, the Husband's other visitation rights notwithstanding;

(x) for the first day of Yom Kippur in every odd-numbered year from 8:30 P.M. until 7:30 P.M.; provided that the Wife shall have the children with her for this same period of time in every even-numbered year, the Husband's other visitation rights notwithstanding;

(y) for Sukkoth in every even-numbered year from 7:30 P.M. on the previous day until 7:30 P.M. of Sukkoth; provided that the Wife shall have the children with her for this same period of time in every odd-numbered year, the Husband's other visitation rights notwithstanding;

(z) for Halloween in every odd-numbered year from 5:30 P.M. until 8:00 P.M.; provided that the Wife shall have the children with her for this same period of time in every even-numbered year, the Husband's other visitation rights notwithstanding;

(aa) on _____, each year from 7:30 P.M. until 9:30 P.M. for the younger child's birthday; provided that the children shall spend the following day with the Wife each year, the Husband's other visitation rights notwithstanding;

(bb) on December 24 from 7:30 P.M. until 10:00 P.M. on December 25 in every odd-numbered year; provided that the Wife shall have the children with her for this same period of time in every even-numbered year, the Husband's other visitation rights notwithstanding;

ITEM 4. CHILD SUPPORT

The Husband shall pay to the Wife the sum of Three Thousand ($3,000.00) Dollars per month for the support, maintenance, and education of the minor children of the parties, (name of Child) and (name of Child), said payments to continue until both children have reached the age of 18 years, married, entered the armed services, or died, whichever combination of events shall first occur, provided that if a child is still attending high school as a full-time student when he or she reaches the age of 18 years, the child support shall continue until the child is graduated or reaches the age of 20 years, whichever first occurs.

Said payments shall be paid on the first day of each month, beginning December 1, 2006, and shall continue on the first day of each month thereafter as hereinabove provided.

In January of each year during which child support is due, beginning January 2006, the Husband shall increase the then current child support payment amount by ten percent (10%), with the first child support payment in the new amount payable February 1.

Whenever, in violation of the terms of this Agreement, there shall have been a failure to make the support payments due hereunder so that the amount unpaid is equal to or greater than the amount payable for one month, the payments required to be made may be collected by the process of continuing garnishment for support.

ITEM 5. ADDITIONAL CHILD SUPPORT

As additional support for the minor children of the parties, the Husband shall provide and pay for four (4) weeks of overnight camp each summer for each child as long as that child wishes to attend summer camp. The Husband shall provide an appropriate Bar Mitzvah for the younger child at the appropriate time.

The Husband shall provide an appropriate wedding and reception for each child.

When each child reaches the age of 16 years, the Husband shall provide that child with an automobile in sound mechanical condition. The Husband shall be responsible for repairs and for the payment of automobile insurance for each vehicle until the Husband's obligation to provide a college education for that child has terminated or been fully satisfied.

ITEM 6. MEDICAL AND DENTAL EXPENSES

The Husband shall provide medical and dental insurance for the children of the parties, at least comparable to that which is now in effect, for as long as each child remains eligible for coverage under the policy terms. The Husband shall also pay all medical, dental, hospital, X-ray, surgery, rehabilitation, nursing, ambulance, orthodontics, psychiatric, prescription drugs or eyeglasses, counseling, chiropractic or any other treatment prescribed, authorized, approved, or rendered by an attending physician or any person licensed by the state of Georgia to practice a healing art incurred for a child while that child remains a minor that are not covered or paid for by said insurance policies.

ITEM 7. COLLEGE EDUCATIONS

The Husband shall pay all expenses incurred by each of the children while under the age of 25 years to secure a four-year college education, or its equivalent, which shall include tuition, books, matriculation fees, room and board, sorority or fraternity expenses, and all other incidental expenses; however, the Husband's obligation hereunder shall be limited to the costs then required for a state resident student to attend the University of Georgia in Athens, Georgia.

ITEM 8. MARITAL PROPERTY

The parties shall divide the property listed below as follows:

(a) The real property located at 0000 _____ Drive, _____ Georgia 00000, is presently titled to the parties as tenants in common. Contemporaneously with the execution of this Agreement, the Husband shall convey, by quitclaim deed to the Wife, all of his right, title, and interest in and to said property. Thereafter, the Wife shall hold said property free of all claims of the Husband and the Wife shall assume, pay in a timely manner, and indemnify and hold the Husband harmless from any obligation for the indebtedness secured by the mortgage on said property;

(b) The 2006 Oldsmobile automobile shall go to the Husband free of all claims of the Wife;

(c) The 2004 vehicle shall go to the Wife, free of all claims of the Husband;

(d) The Husband shall have all issued and outstanding shares of _____, Inc. free of all claims of the Wife;

(e) The Husband's Individual Retirement Accounts shall go to the Wife, who shall thereafter hold said accounts free of all claims of the Husband;

(f) The _____ life insurance policy that insures the Husband's life in the amount of Two Hundred Thousand ($200,000) Dollars shall be assigned to the Wife, who shall thereafter be the owner of said policy and responsible for all premiums thereon as long as the Wife elects to maintain said policy;

(g) Except as otherwise provided herein, all checking accounts, savings accounts, credit union accounts, money market accounts, Individual Retirement Accounts, pension and profit-sharing accounts, 401(k) accounts, other retirement accounts, insurance policies, stocks, bonds, and other tangible or intangible property titled in the name of either party on the date of the execution of this Agreement shall be the sole property of that party, and the other shall have no claim thereto;

(h) Except as otherwise provided herein, the parties have made an amicable division of their marital property, including but not limited to household furniture, furnishings, and personal effects, and neither party shall claim any property in the possession of the other party on the date of the signing of this Agreement;

(i) Each party shall promptly sign all documents and forms, upon request, which are required by any bank, transfer agent, or other institution necessary to change title to the above accounts and securities consistent with this Agreement.

ITEM 9. DEBTS OF THE MARRIAGE

The Husband shall be responsible for and pay in a timely manner all debts that were incurred by the parties prior to the execution of this Agreement and shall hold the Wife harmless from any liability therefore. Each party shall be responsible for and pay in a timely manner any and all debts incurred in his or her name after the execution of this Agreement and shall hold the other party harmless therefrom.

ITEM 10. ALIMONY

The Husband shall pay to the Wife for her support the sum of One Thousand ($1,000) Dollars per month until the Wife dies, or until thirty-six (36) such payments have been paid, whichever event shall first occur. These payments shall be paid on the first day of each month, beginning December 1, 2006, and shall continue on the first day of each month thereafter as hereinabove provided.

ITEM 11. ANNUAL BOAT SHOW

The Husband shall provide an entry card to the boat show held annually in Atlanta to the Wife. The Wife shall be solely responsible for any costs or charges associated with her attendance at the show.

ITEM 12. LIFE INSURANCE

The Husband shall maintain a minimum of Two Hundred Fifty Thousand ($250,000.00) Dollars of unencumbered life insurance on his life, with the Wife named as irrevocable beneficiary. The life insurance policies shall be kept in full force until all obligations required of the Husband under the terms of this Agreement have terminated

The Husband shall provide a copy of the policy or policies that provide this coverage to the Wife and shall instruct the company providing this coverage to notify the Wife of each premium when due. The Husband shall also provide written evidence to the Wife at least annually that said insurance is unencumbered and otherwise in effect.

If the Husband should die while retaining an obligation under this Item to provide life insurance to the Wife, and if the Wife, as beneficiary, does not receive the amount of insurance to which she is otherwise entitled hereunder, then the difference between the amount to which the Wife is entitled hereunder and the amount she actually receives, if any, shall be a first charge against the Husband's estate, and the Husband's administrators, executors, and trustees are hereby directed to pay said sum to the Wife, provisions of the Husband's Last Will and Testament to the contrary notwithstanding.

ITEM 13. INCOME TAX INDEMNIFICATION

The Husband shall indemnify and hold the Wife harmless from all deficiencies, including penalties and interest thereon, arising out of or relating to any and all joint state and federal income tax returns signed and filed by the parties during the term of the marriage. The Husband shall defend, at his sole cost and expenses, all attempts to impose any assessments and collect the same against or from the Wife and any property of the Wife. Should the Husband fail to perform his obligations hereunder, the Wife shall be entitled to recover from the Husband all losses and assessments, together with all costs and expenses including attorneys' fees and accountants' fees which she may owe, incur, or pay as a result of the Husband's failure to comply with this ITEM.

ITEM 14. DISCOVERY WAIVER

Each party acknowledges that procedures are available under the Georgia Civil Practice Act to fully inquire into and investigate the assets, income, and liabilities of the other party before considering any settlement in this matter, Each party further acknowledges that those procedures have not been fully utilized and that this Agreement has been negotiated and reached without the benefit of full discovery. Each party hereby specifically waives her or his rights to additional discovery and accepts the terms set out in this Agreement in full satisfaction of all rights and claims against the other party.

ITEM 15. UNDERSTANDING AND ASSENT

The parties acknowledge that they are entering into this Agreement freely and voluntarily; that they have made a full disclosure of all facts that may be relevant to this Agreement to the other; that they have arrived at the terms of this Agreement through the process of negotiation through counsel; that they have ascertained and weighed all of the facts and circumstances likely to influence their legal decisions independently of the other; that they have each been provided the opportunity to review this Agreement with counsel independently of the other; that they have each given due consideration to the provisions contained within this Agreement; and that they clearly understand and assent to all of the provisions hereof.

IN WITNESS WHEREOF, the parties have signed their names and affixed their seals to three counterparts of this Agreement, each of which shall be enforceable as an original, this _____ day of October, 2006.

_____
Wife

Sworn to and subscribed
before me this, the _____
day of November, 2006.

_____
Notary Public

_____
Husband

Sworn to and subscribed
before me this, the _____
day of November, 2006.

_____
Notary Public

Example of Settlement Agreement—No Children

IN THE SUPERIOR COURT OF _____ COUNTY
STATE OF GEORGIA

_____,)

Plaintiff,

vs.

_____,)

Defendant,

)
)
)
)
) CIVIL ACTION FILE
) NO. 000000000
)
)

SEPARATION AGREEMENT

This Agreement, made and entered into by and between _____
(hereinafter referred to as "Wife"), and _____, (hereinafter referred to as "Husband"):

WITNESSETH:

WHEREAS, Husband and Wife were married on June 1, 19__; and

WHEREAS, no children were born as issue of the marriage nor are any
expected; and

WHEREAS, neither party to this Agreement is laboring under any
disabilities at law; and

WHEREAS, unfortunate differences have arisen between the parties, as
a result of which Husband and Wife have agreed to separate and live apart
from each other in a bona fide state of separation; and

WHEREAS, Husband and Wife wish to settle all issues as to alimony,
division of property, payment of debts, and all other issues between them;

NOW, THEREFORE, in consideration of the covenants, promises,
Agreements, and other valuable considerations that are hereinafter set forth,
the parties agree as follows:

ITEM 1. FUTURE RELATIONSHIP OF HUSBAND AND WIFE

Husband and Wife shall continue to live separate and apart and each
shall be free from the interference, authority, and control, either direct or
indirect, of the other, except as may be otherwise expressly provided hereinafter in this agreement without regard to any other provisions hereof, each

may reside at such place or places as he or she may deem appropriate and each may, for his or her own separate use or benefit, engage in any employment, business or profession that he or she may deem advisable.

The Wife is hereby restrained and enjoined from coming within two hundred (200) yards of the marital residence after 3:00 P.M. on November 13, 2006. The Husband is hereby restrained and enjoined from coming within two hundred (200) yards of the Wife's residence or ABC Inc. offices after 3:00 P.M. on November 13, 2006.

ITEM 2. ALIMONY

The Wife shall pay to the Husband for his support and maintenance the sum of Ten Thousand Dollars ($10,000.00) per month, said payments to continue until the Husband dies, the Wife dies, or until one hundred twenty (120) such payments have been paid, whichever event shall first occur. The Wife shall pay the first of said payments on the third day of the first month following the execution of this Agreement and shall continue to make payments on the third day of each month thereafter until the alimony obligation terminates as provided by this ITEM.

The provisions for alimony as hereinabove set out shall be subject to an action for modification only under the terms and conditions set out in O.C.G.A. Section 19-6-19(a), based upon a change in the income and financial status of the Wife. The provisions for alimony as hereinabove set out shall not be subject to modification because of a change in the income and financial status of the Husband, the remarriage of the Husband, or under the provisions of O.C.G.A. Section 19-6-19(b), and each party hereby specifically waives the right to seek a modification of alimony because of the Husband's possible remarriage or voluntary cohabitation with a third party in any type of relationship.

The payments set out in this ITEM shall be deductible as alimony to the Wife and taxable to the Husband under the Internal Revenue Code of 1986, as amended, and neither party shall take a position on his or her income tax returns that is inconsistent with this provision.

ITEM 3. TAX DEFICIENCIES

The Husband hereby indemnifies the Wife against all liability for taxes and penalties and interest thereon as finally determined and assessed against the Wife, or the Wife and Husband jointly, arising out of or resulting from any income or deduction item entered on any joint income tax return signed and filed by the parties during the term of the marriage that is attributable to the Husband's business activities.

The Wife hereby indemnifies the Husband against all liability for taxes and penalties and interest thereon as finally determined and assessed against the Husband, or the Wife and Husband jointly, arising out of or resulting

from any income or deduction item entered on any joint income tax return signed and filed by the parties during the term of the marriage that is attributable to the Wife's business activities,

Should any tax liability to which such indemnity applies be proposed or determined against the parties, they shall:

(a) promptly notify the other party or the other party's estate of such proposals or determinations, furnish detail of such proposals or determinations, including a copy of the writing, if any, by which such liability is proposed or determined, and determine which party is obligated hereunder to assume responsibility for the matter; and

(b) permit the other party or the other party's estate at his, hers or its expense to defend against such proposals or determinations; provided, however, that should the obligated party or his or her estate decline to defend the other party against such proposals or determinations, then the obligated party or his or her estate shall indemnify the other party against expenses and reasonable attorney fees incurred in defending such proposals or determinations, as well as the amount of any tax deficiencies, including penalties and interest thereon, as finally determined. Each party hereby represents to the other that he or she has received no notice of deficiency or audit notice for their joint returns from the Internal Revenue Service or from any Department of Revenue or other such department of any state and that all taxes shown as due on joint income tax returns previously filed have been paid.

Each party is and shall be the custodian of certain of the records and documents that provide the substantiation for the entries on the parties' joint income tax returns for calendar tax years 1990 through 2005. Each party shall continue to maintain those records for the benefit of both parties, and if at any time one party requires documents from the other, then upon fifteen (15) days' notice to the other party, the other party shall provide same to the requesting party.

<u>ITEM 4. REAL PROPERTY</u>

The parties shall dispose of the real property located at 000 _____ Way, _____, _____ County, Georgia, presently titled to the parties as tenants in common as follows. Contemporaneously with the execution of this Agreement, the Wife shall convey by limited warranty deed, subject only to the existing first deed to secure debt, all of her right, title, and interest in said property to the Husband. The Wife hereby warrants to the Husband that she has caused no other liens or encumbrances to be placed against the property. In the event other liens or encumbrances have been placed against the property by the Wife, the Wife shall be solely responsible for and timely pay all payments on said liens and encumbrances on said property and shall indemnify and hold the Husband harmless from any liability therefor.

After the payment due in December 2006 has been paid by the Wife, the Husband shall assume and be solely responsible for and timely pay all payments on the note that is secured by a mortgage on said property and shall indemnify and hold the Wife harmless from any liability therefore. The Husband hereby warrants to the Wife that he has caused no other liens or encumbrances to be placed against the property. In the event other liens or encumbrances have been placed against the property by the Husband, the Husband shall be solely responsible for and timely pay all payments on said liens and encumbrances on said property and shall indemnify and hold the Wife harmless from any liability therefor.

The Husband shall also take all steps necessary to refinance the note prior to the time the balloon payment on the note, which is secured by said property, becomes due, thus releasing the Wife from all potential liability thereon. The home equity line with _____ Bank has been paid in full by the Husband and neither party shall make any further borrowings on this line, and said line shall be cancelled. The Husband shall have the right to exclusive possession of said property as of 3:00 P.M. November 13, 2006.

The Wife shall pay the expenses to carry the mortgage through December and shall be entitled to claim all income tax deductions relating to all mortgage payments paid in 2006. Except as otherwise provided herein regarding the mortgage payment, the Wife shall pay all expenses incurred by her in connection with her sole possession of the home since March 25, 2006 through November 30, 2006, including but not limited to mortgage payments, utility payments, repairs, maintenance and landscaping, new carpet, re-keyed locks, improvements made by the Wife, and telephone and AT&T bills. Bills and statements that arrive after November 30, 2006, shall be prorated and the Wife shall provide a copy of the most recent bill paid by her and promptly reimburse the Husband for her pro-rata share. At or before 3:00 P.M. on November 13, 2006, the Wife shall deliver possession of the home to the Husband in the same condition in which he left it March 25, 2006, normal wear and tear excepted.

The Wife shall thereafter have no further access to the property. When possession of the home is transferred from the Wife to the Husband, the Wife shall also deliver all keys and garage door openers to the Husband. The Wife shall give the Husband the current security code. She will also call _____ Security Company, instruct the company to remove her name from the account and further instruct them that the Husband will be calling to change the code and that he does so with her approval.

The Wife shall deliver to the Husband all documents and records in her possession that relate to improvements made to said property.

ITEM 5. PERSONAL PROPERTY

The parties shall divide the personal property acquired by them during the term of the marriage as follows:

(a) The 2006 Mercedes automobile shall go to the Wife free of all claims of the Husband, and the Husband shall sign over the title to the Wife contemporaneously with the signing of this Agreement;

(b) The 2006 Buick automobile shall go to the Husband free of all claims of the Wife and free of all encumbrances. The Wife shall sign over the title to the Husband contemporaneously with the signing of this Agreement. The Wife shall pay the ad valorem tax for said vehicle prior to November 2, 2006;

(c) The furniture and personal property set out on Exhibit A to this Agreement, and only those items, shall go to the Wife, who shall remove said property from the marital residence prior to the final inspection by the Husband;

(d) The following assets shall go to the Husband, free of all claims of the Wife:

(1) _____ Bond and the _____account;

(2) All _____ accounts titled to either party;

(3) Any Money Market Accounts;

(4) All retirement accounts titled in the name of either party

(5) _____Stock;

(6) Any interest in any trust of which the Husband is a trustee or beneficiary;

(7) All retirement accounts titled in the name of either party, including but not limited to:

    (A) _____ Individual Retirement Account titled to Wife;

    (B) _____ Individual Retirement Account titled to Wife;

    (C) _____ Individual Retirement Account titled to Wife;

    (D) _____ Individual Retirement Account titled to Wife;

    (E) ABC, Inc. 401(k) Account titled to Wife;

(8) To the extent any of the above-listed assets have been frozen, the Wife shall immediately cooperate to the extent required to transfer said assets to the Husband unencumbered and prior to November 17, 2006;

(9) The Husband shall be solely responsible for all tax liabilities arising out of or associated with any of the assets listed above in subparagraph (7) of this Item 5.

(e) All original documents which form substantiation for the parties' joint income tax returns as well as all additional documents produced by the Wife in response to the Husband's discovery requests but excluding documents that relate directly to ABC, Inc. shall go to the Husband;

(f) Except for the items set out on Exhibit A hereto, all furniture, furnishings, and personal property now in the marital residence shall go to the Husband, free of all claims of the Wife;

(g) The furniture and personal property set out in Exhibit B, now at the Wife's office, shall go to the Husband, and the Wife shall return said items to the marital residence by November 13, 2006;

(h) The Wife shall retain, free of all claims of the Husband, all of her right, title, and interest inABC, Incorporated, and the Wife shall indemnify and hold Husband harmless from any claims associated with ABC, Incorporated;

(i) The Husband shall retain, free of all claims of the Wife, all of his right, title, and interest in _____ Company and the Husband shall indemnify and hold the Wife harmless from any claims associated with _____ Company;

(j) The Wife shall transfer to the Husband a total of Two Hundred Fifty Thousand (250,000) Delta Frequent Flyer Miles. The Wife shall accomplish this by adding the Husband's name to her credit card account. She shall then transfer the miles to the Husband's Frequent Flyer Account Number 00000000000 under the name of Husband. Once the transfer is complete, the Wife may remove the Husband from the credit card account;

(k) Each party shall own any and all life insurance policies that insure that party's life, including all cash values therein, free of all claims of the other;

(l) Except as otherwise provided elsewhere in this Agreement, all checking accounts, savings accounts, credit union accounts, money market accounts, Individual Retirement Accounts, life insurance policies (including cash values thereof), pension and profit-sharing accounts, stocks, bonds, and other tangible or intangible property titled in the name of either party on the date this Agreement is signed shall be the sole property of that party and the other shall have no claim thereto;

(m) Except as otherwise provided herein, the parties have made an amicable division of their marital property, including but not limited to household furniture, furnishings, and personal effects, and neither party shall claim any tangible property in the possession of the other party on the date this Agreement is signed;

(n) Each party shall promptly sign all documents and forms, upon request, that are required by any bank, transfer agent, or other institution necessary to change title to the above property consistent with this Agreement. Upon the failure of either party to execute or deliver any such deed, bill of sale, endorsement, form, conveyance, or other document to the other party, this Agreement shall constitute and operate as such properly executed document. The County Clerk and any and all other public and commercial officials are authorized and directed to accept this Agreement, or a properly certified copy thereof, in lieu of the document regularly required for the conveyance or transfer.

ITEM 6. QUALIFIED DOMESTIC RELATIONS ORDER

The parties acknowledge that, as part of the division of marital assets set out in ITEM 4 above, the Wife is transferring to the Husband the balances of all of her retirement accounts, as more fully described above in ITEM 5(d)(7)(A), (B), (C), (D), and (E) as of the date of final transfer. The transfers of these accounts shall be effectuated by having qualified domestic relations orders, where necessary, which meet all of the ERISA requirements and which have been approved by the plan administrators where required, entered by the Superior Court of _____ County, Georgia, at the earliest possible time. The parties agree that the Superior Court of _____ County, Georgia, shall retain jurisdiction as necessary in order to carry out the provisions of this ITEM.

The parties acknowledge that this transfer of retirement funds is and shall be a portion of the property settlement and not alimony from the Wife to the Husband.

ITEM 7. DEBTS OF THE MARRIAGE

The Wife shall be solely responsible for the repayment of her loan to ABC, Incorporated and shall indemnify and hold the Husband harmless from any liability therefor.

The Husband shall be solely responsible for the repayment of all loans of the parties and ABC, Incorporated from Dr. _____ and shall indemnify and hold the Wife harmless from any liability therefor. Based on representations made by Dr. _____, there are no outstanding loans from ABC, Incorporated to Dr._____.

Except for the note secured by the marital residence and as otherwise provided herein, the parties acknowledge that there are no joint unpaid debts of the marriage. Except as otherwise provided herein, each party shall be solely responsible for and pay any and all debts incurred in his or her name, and shall indemnify and hold the other party harmless therefrom.

ITEM 8. LIFE INSURANCE ON WIFE'S LIFE

CHAPTER

14

Settlements

The Wife shall maintain reducing-term life insurance on her life, in effect and unencumbered, with the Husband named as irrevocable beneficiary, until all of the Wife's obligations for payment of alimony to the Husband set out in ITEM 2 of this Agreement have been fully satisfied or terminated. At all times, the amount of life insurance provided shall be sufficient to fully pay the Wife's outstanding alimony obligation at the time of her death, reduced to then present value (hereinafter "Life Insurance Obligation Amount"). The Wife shall provide copies of the policies and beneficiary designations that provide this coverage to the Husband. Upon written request of the Husband, but no more often than once each calendar year, the Wife shall provide written proof to the Husband that the amount of insurance required hereunder is unencumbered and otherwise currently in effect.

In the event the Wife should die with an obligation for alimony outstanding and in the Amount, then the difference between the amount of insurance proceeds left to the Husband, if any, and the Life Insurance Obligation Amount shall be a first charge against the Wife's estate, and the Executors, Administrators, and personal representatives of the Wife's estate are hereby directed to pay this difference to the Husband before the payment of other creditors of the estate, provisions of the Wife's last will and testament to the contrary notwithstanding.

ITEM 9. ABC INCORPORATED

The parties acknowledge that the Husband was an employee of ABC, Incorporated (hereinafter "ABC") through October 31, 2006, at which time his employment terminated. In the event the Husband shall apply for disability income under the ABC group policy, the Wife shall promptly cooperate and facilitate the processing of the claim for the employer as the vice-president of ABC.

The parties acknowledge that all matters relating to his employment are set out in a certain Agreement between the Husband and ABC. The Wife, as owner of one-half (1/2) of the issued and outstanding shares of the company and as vice-president of ABC, hereby guarantees that the obligations of ABC set out in that Agreement will be carried out.

ITEM 10. ATTORNEYS' FEES

Each party shall pay his or her own attorneys' fees and expenses of litigation incurred in connection with this matter and make no claim against the other party for any contribution thereto.

ITEM 11. MODIFICATION

Except as otherwise specifically provided herein, no modification or waiver of any of the terms of this Agreement shall be valid unless in writing and signed by both parties.

ITEM 12. WAIVER OF BREACH

The waiver of any breach of this Agreement shall not constitute a continuing waiver or waiver of any subsequent breach, whether of the same or of a different provision of this Agreement.

ITEM 13. LEGAL CONSTRUCTION

In case any one or more of the provisions contained in this Agreement shall, for any reason, be held to be invalid, illegal, or unenforceable in any respect, such invalidity, illegality, or unenforceability shall not affect any other provision hereof and this Agreement shall be construed as if such invalid, illegal, or unenforceable provision had never been contained herein.

This Agreement is filed in this action brought by the Wife as a resident of the state of Georgia against the Husband who continues to be a resident of the state of Georgia, and the parties agree that any interpretation or legal construction of this Agreement shall be governed by Georgia law.

ITEM 14. WAIVER

Each party hereby waives any and all claims he or she may hereafter have against the other upon or by reason or any matter, cause or thing up to the date of the execution of this Agreement, except as to the obligations set out in this Agreement.

ITEM 15. NOTICES

All notices, requests, demands, and other communications required hereunder shall be in writing and shall be deemed to have been duly given if delivered personally, by telecopy, by telefax, by electronic mail, or, if mailed, by United States Certified mail to the other party at that party's last known address.

ITEM 16. TAX CONSEQUENCES

The Husband and Wife have been advised, prior to the execution of this Agreement, to seek from competent Certified Public Accountants (C.P.A.) or other tax consultants all advice regarding taxes and the tax impact of the provisions of this Agreement, and for such other advice and filings as may be appropriate under the circumstances; and the Husband and Wife further understand that any documents, reports or elections to be filed pursuant to such advice must be filed by the parties or by the C.P.A. or other tax consultant engaged by a party.

Each party is aware that there may be certain tax consequences associated with this Agreement or as a result of their entering into this Agreement. Each party understands that, prior to the execution of this Agreement, he or she should consult with a C.P.A. to satisfy himself or herself of any tax consequences that may result from this Agreement.

ITEM 17. DISCOVERY

Before this Agreement was negotiated, each party had the opportunity to or was advised of his or her rights under the Georgia Civil Practice to conduct formal discovery, investigation, and analysis of the assets, liabilities, income and conduct of the other party. Each party hereby knowingly and voluntarily chooses to forgo his and/or her rights and to accept the provisions of this Agreement on the basis of information acquired informally, without formal discovery

ITEM 18. LEGAL ADVICE

Each party expressly acknowledges that he or she has consulted with counsel of his or her choice, or had the opportunity to do so, and has been duly apprised of his or her respective legal rights, and that all questions pertaining thereto have been fully and satisfactorily explained to that party separately by his or her counsel

ITEM 19. UNDERSTANDING AND ASSENT

The parties each acknowledge that they are entering into this Agreement freely and voluntarily; that they have each made a full disclosure of all facts that may be relevant to this Agreement to the other; that they have arrived at the terms of this Agreement through the process of mediation; that they have each ascertained and weighed all of the facts and circumstances likely to influence their legal decisions independently of the other; that they have each been provided the opportunity to review this Agreement with counsel independently of the other; that they have each given due consideration to the provisions contained within this Agreement; that they have read each page of this Agreement before signing same; that they each believe this Agreement is reasonable under the circumstances; and that they clearly understand and assent to all of the provisions hereof.

Each party further represents and warrants that, at the time this Agreement was negotiated and executed, neither party was under the influence of alcohol, drugs, or any other substance or condition that impaired his or her ability to clearly understand and assent to the provisions of this Agreement.

IN WITNESS WHEREOF, the parties have signed their names and affixed their seals to three counterparts of this Agreement, each of which shall be enforceable as an original, this _____ day of November, 2006.

_____
Wife

Subscribed before me this
___ day of November, 2006

_____
Notary Public

_____
Husband

Subscribed before me this
___ day of November, 2006

_____
Notary Public

Opposing Counsel
Address

      Re: Plaintiff v. Defendant (insert style of case)
          Superior Court of _____ County
          CAFN 12345A

Dear (Opposing Counsel):

      Enclosed please find my Client's 2006 Income Tax Return that was filed in April of 2006.

      My client and I are formulating a Counteroffer to submit in response to your offer of settlement and compromise dated June 1, 2006. However, in an abundance of caution, my client hereby formally rejects the offer submitted by you and your client on June 1, 2006. We will be submitting a Counteroffer shortly that has a more realistic chance of resolving the case.

      Your cooperation is greatly appreciated.

                  Sincerely,

                  Attorney

Letter to Opposing Counsel Regarding Delayed Resolution

Opposing Counsel
Address

Re: Plaintiff v. Defendant
    Superior Court of _____ County
    CAFN 12345A

Dear (Opposing Counsel):

Thank you for your recent letter.

We are concerned about the delay in resolution and hope that this does not mean that your client is thinking of revising the substantive terms of the Agreement. Because I am concerned about this, given the delay, I wanted to make sure that we preserve the tape-recording of the settlement that the mediator gave to you. Would you please save the tape and have it transcribed?

My client has indicated to me that she will be in Atlanta on July 30 and July 31, 2006, and we would like to have the matter wrapped up by then.

I understand that your client has had family reunions and vacations that have delayed his attention to this matter. I would appreciate it if you would provide me two dates: (1) when can we expect to see the revisions to the Agreement; and (2) when I might get the transcript of the settlement tape from you. If you do not anticipate being able to get that transcript to me by July 20, 2006, please let me know so that I can make arrangements to have it transcribed. If necessary, we will do it in your office to assure your client of security.

Thank you for your assistance.

Very truly yours,

Attorney

Letter to Opposing Counsel with Follow-Up Items

Opposing Counsel
Address

Re: Plaintiff v. Defendant
Superior Court of _____ County
CAFN 12345A

Dear (Opposing Counsel):

Enclosed you will find several items:

1. Triplicate originals of the revised Agreement, each of which has been signed by my client. I am assuming from our telephone conversations that this document will be acceptable to your client. If there are any problems, please let me know immediately.

2. A letter of authorization to ABC Inc. This relates to the _____ bond. Please have your client sign this in the bottom right-hand corner.

3. A voided deposit slip for my client's account at _____Bank. I am supplying this in the event your client would like to set up a direct deposit for the monthly spousal support payments.

Within the next couple of days I will forward the following:

A. A Qualified Domestic Relations Order for the transfer of the 401(k) account.

B. The Limited Warranty Deed to the marital residence for your client's signature, if you will provide me with a legal description.

C. The _____ transfer documents. Your client's signature will need to be guaranteed by a bank officer.

D. Information on the recipient IRA for those transfers.

In order to unfreeze the _____ Bank money market account, your client will need to see Mr. Jones at the Bank to sign the required documents. Perhaps she could get her signature guaranteed on the _____ document at that time.

We propose that your client leave the house keys, garage door openers, and information concerning the current security code at the home of the neighbor, _____. My client can then retrieve those items next Friday afternoon after 3:00 P.M.

Finally, enclosed is a copy of a letter I have sent to Judge _____, taking this case off the November 13 calendar and resetting it to the November 17 calendar. I am hopeful that Judge _____ will be able to enter a final decree on that day. If you have any questions or if I have omitted anything, please let me know at your earliest opportunity. I look forward to hearing from you.

Very truly yours,

Attorney

Closing Matters

Eventually all things come to an end, even divorce cases. We hope it is because of a reasonable settlement and a contented client. Whatever the sentiment, it is time to finish up. This is when you should go through the file and return all original documents to your client. This is also when you should accompany the return of the documents with a closing letter. The letter should summarize that the divorce is final, what the appeals rights are, what happens with wills, and similar items. It should also make clear that your job is done and that any further work by you for the client will be based on a new relationship and new fees.

Letter to Get Information for Funds Transfer Under a
Qualified Domestic Relations Order

_____ Bank

Address

Re: Individual Retirement Account #1111111111
_____, Plaintiff

Plaintiff v. Defendant
Superior Court of _____ County
CAFN 12345A

Dear Sir or Madam:

I am writing on behalf of my client, _____. As part of a settlement in the above-referenced case, her spouse, _____, has agreed to transfer his IRA to her. The purpose of this letter is to ask that you send any forms or instructions used by _____ Bank to accomplish this transfer. Once the paperwork is complete and the Qualified Domestic Relations Order is entered, we would like to complete this transfer in a timely manner.

Of course, it you have questions, or if I can provide additional assistance, please let me know.

Thank you for your assistance with this matter.

Sincerely,

Attorney

_____ Bank

Address

     Re: Individual Retirement Account #1111111111

     _____, Plaintiff

Plaintiff v. Defendant

Superior Court of _____ County

CAFN 12345A

Dear Sir or Madam:

    Enclosed you will find an Qualified Domestic Relations Order, which transfers the above-referenced account from _____, Plaintiff to my client, _____, Defendant. Please treat this as an IRA Rollover and transfer it directly to Defendant's IRA Account # 22222222222 at _____Brokerage Company. If particular forms are required, please send them to me at your earliest convenience. Of course, if you have questions or if I can provide additional assistance, please let me know.

    Thank you for your assistance with this matter.

                      Sincerely,

                      Attorney

Final Summary Letter to Client

Client
Address

Re: Plaintiff v. Defendant
    Superior Court of _____ County
    CAFN 12345A

Dear (Client):

The purpose of this letter is to summarize the current status of your divorce case. As you know, you and your spouse signed a Settlement Agreement last week. He and his attorney went to Court yesterday, June 1, 2006, for the final hearing. The Judge granted the divorce and incorporated the Settlement Agreement into the Final Divorce Decree. This means that everything in the Agreement is also now part of a Court Order and can be enforced through Contempt of Court proceedings should one of you fail to abide by the Agreement terms. Enclosed is a certified copy of the Final Divorce Decree.

Even though the date of the divorce is yesterday, and, for all intents and purposes, the divorce is final, in the event either of you were to decide to appeal the case for any reason, there is a 30-day period that began yesterday during which the appeal could be filed. Once that time has run, the divorce is completely final.

The Final Divorce Decree also restored you to your maiden name, _____. At this point, you need to begin the process of changing your name on your driver's license, Social Security account, passport, bank accounts, brokerage accounts, credit cards, etc. A photocopy of the Decree should be sufficient, but if you need additional certified copies, you can get them in the Clerk's office at the courthouse.

If you had a will that you signed during the marriage, it is now void by operation of Georgia law unless it specifically contemplated and made reference to the divorce. Should you die before you sign a new will, your two children would be your heirs at law, but even though they would inherit your estate, it would be much better for them if you have a valid will in place. I suggest you put this at the top of your "to-do" list.

Because your spouse agreed to transfer his Individual Retirement Account to you, the Judge also signed a Qualified Domestic Relations Order, a copy of which is enclosed. I have already sent that to _____ Bank, asking that his IRA be rolled over to your IRA at the _____ Bank. That process should be completed shortly, and I will let you know when it is finished.

As you know, your now ex-spouse has agreed to pay $5,000 of your attorneys' fees at the rate of $1,000 per month. Each payment we receive will be applied to the outstanding balance of your bill and, after all of his payments have been received, you will be entitled to a refund of any remainder.

I know this was a long and sometimes frustrating experience for you but I believe the overall result is a good one. I enjoyed working with you; you were a very good client and I appreciate that. I hope things go well for you in the future.

Best wishes,

Attorney

CHAPTER

15

LETTERS FOR
DIVORCE
LAWYERS

Opposing Counsel
Address

Re: Plaintiff v. Defendant

Dear (Opposing Counsel):

Enclosed please find a copy of the Final Judgment and Decree as entered by the Clerk in the above-referenced case. I believe all the furniture has been divided and other details between our clients have been sorted out. I am glad we were able to successfully resolve this case and I enjoyed working with you and your staff. I look forward to a similar opportunity in the near future.

Sincerely,

Attorney

Short Close-Out Letter to Client

Client
Address

Re: Plaintiff v. Defendant

Dear (Client):

Enclosed please find your copy of the Agreement and the Final Consent Order signed by the Judge. I am certainly glad we were able to reach a satisfactory conclusion to this. I believer there are certain features in the Agreement that will prove to be most beneficial over time. I enjoyed working with you in this matter.

I will settle up your account when the September bills are prepared early in October and will refund any balance of the retainer.

Best wishes to you.

Sincerely,

Attorney

Prenuptial Agreements

T hese are increasingly popular. Often these agreements come about where one party is much better off financially than the other. If you are called upon to represent one party with pre-marital planning, it is essential that your client make a full disclosure of his/her financial circumstances, especially if your client is the one with the significant assets. Prenuptial agreements also come up when the parties are older and have children from prior marriages. The difficult part is figuring out how to handle different contingencies; however, once that is done, drafting the document is relatively simple. Be aware that occasionally the stress of working through this less than romantic task will actually end the marriage before it starts.

Letter to Client with Overview of Proposed Prenuptial Agreement
Prepared by Other Attorney

Client
Address

Dear (Client):

After reviewing the proposed Agreement prepared by your Fiancé's attorney and my notes from our conference on March 5, I see that the Agreement seeks to address three areas:

1. During the marriage;
2   In the event of divorce;
3   In the event of death.

Based on our conference and my notes, I believe we tentatively arrived at the following preferred terms in each situation:

1. <u>During the marriage</u>: During the marriage, Fiancé will be responsible for the direct housing expenses, including mortgage, insurance, property taxes, utilities. Fiancé will also deposit the sum of "X" into a joint account on the first day of each month. You will be responsible for staffing the marital residence as necessary for cleaning, pool maintenance, lawn maintenance, and other similar services. Those expenses will be paid from the joint account. You will also use that account to pay miscellaneous expenses such as groceries, dry cleaning, etc. The monthly amount deposited into this account will be adjusted no less frequently than annually, taking into consideration the ongoing expenses paid from the account and the annual inflation increase. The amount deposited to this account will be paid regardless of your working status. Of course, you will need to determine the value of "X."

Fiancé will also provide you with an automobile no less frequently than every two years and comparable to a new Mercedes 500 series automobile.

2. <u>In the event of a divorce</u>: For purposes of the Agreement, a divorce will be considered initiated if either of you actually files a divorce complaint in the appropriate court and has the other served with a copy of the divorce complaint. If you file the divorce complaint, then the provisions set out in Item 2.1.5 on page 4 of the proposed Agreement will be in effect.

If Fiancé initiates the divorce by filing a divorce complaint, then you will receive an amount equal to the greater of a percentage of the net worth of Fiancé's separate property or a fixed dollar sum, determined as follows:

Less than two years of marriage: 5% or $500,000
Two years of marriage: 10% or $525,000
Three years of marriage: 15% or $550,000
Four years of marriage: 20% or $575,000
Five years of marriage: 25% or $600,000
Six years of marriage: 30% or $625,000
Seven or more years of marriage   33.33% or $650,000

In either event Fiancé will keep his separate property and the marital residence. You will keep your separate property, personal property, automobile, and the property settlement amount.

3. Death: If you predecease Fiancé, he will be entitled to one-half (1/2) of your estate as itemized for federal estate tax purposes and not probate purposes. It will be his option to renounce his interest in your estate in favor of your children.

In the event Fiancé predeceases you, he will leave you one-third (1/3) of his estate, itemized for federal estate tax purposes and not probate purposes.

As we discussed, you are not particularly interested in keeping the marital residence, although you might change your mind at a later time. We discussed the possibility that Fiancé could give you the right to include the home, free of all debt, in your share of Fiancé's estate if you wished. We also discussed that, in any event, you should have the right to live in the home during the probate process and should have control over the sale of the home.

As an alternative, we discussed leaving the home in the estate and providing that assets, such as Fiancé's life insurance proceeds and his Individual Retirement Accounts, go directly to you and that you receive only the balance of your one-third (1/3) of the estate from home proceeds or other estate assets. The advantage of this alternative would be to guarantee you certain funds immediately, with minimum input from the other beneficiaries of Fiancé's probate estate.

In order for the Agreement to be useful, it must be as specific as possible, but also must be flexible enough to include increases, decreases, and changes in circumstances and assets during the course of the marriage.

For instance, it is not necessary to have a precise value on Fiancé's business (or anything else) at this time, but it is necessary to know what happens to the business and other assets in the event of death or divorce.

After you have reviewed this and given it more thought, please give me a call so that we can discuss this in detail.

I look forward to hearing from you.

Very truly yours,

Attorney

Transmittal Letter to Client with Summary Overview
of Proposed Prenuptial Agreement

CHAPTER

16

Prenuptial
Agreements

Client
Address

Dear (Client):

   I have reviewed the draft agreement and am enclosing a summary of
the major points. After you have reviewed this, give me a call and we can
discuss possible next steps. I look forward to hearing from you.

                                        Sincerely,

                                    Attorney

SUMMARY OF DRAFT AGREEMENT

SECTION 1 You are not now married, you are making a full disclosure of your assets and liabilities, you are voluntarily entering into the Agreement, and you will cooperate in carrying out the terms of the Agreement.

SECTION 2 Separate <u>property</u> consists of all assets acquired before marriage and by inheritance or gift at any time, along with its income and profits, and belongs to the party acquiring it. In the event of divorce, Fiancé agrees to give you the lesser of a fixed dollar amount or a percentage of his separate property based on the duration of the marriage. <u>Property acquired after marriage</u> will belong to you in proportion to your respective contributions.

<u>Principal residence</u> shall be owned as tenants in common in proportion to your initial contributions to its purchase. Fiancé agrees to assume responsibility for any loan and to pay all expenses. If you divorce, Fiancé has a right to buy your interest, or if he does not elect to do so, you then have the right to buy Fiancé's interest. <u>If Fiancé dies while you are married, he agrees to give you his interest in the home, subject to any loans.</u>

SECTION 3 <u>Provisions during marriage</u>: Fiancé agrees that, at his death, he will leave you the home and furnishings and to create a trust for your lifetime with a minimum gift of $1 million. You agree to allow Fiancé to use your annual exclusion. Fiancé also agrees to give you a monthly allowance and to pay all household expenses, furnish you with a car, and provide health insurance and/or pay your uninsured medical expenses.

SECTION 4 Property shall retain its characterization as separate or marital. <u>Each of you can apply time and efforts to separate property without creating marital rights in that property, and can allow the other to use separate property without changing its character</u>. If one of you applies separate or marital property to the other's separate property, that shall not change the character of either type of property and shall not give rise to a right of reimbursement. Each of you retains the right to make gifts to the other.

SECTION 5 Release of any and all claims and rights in and to the property or estate of the other. State support obligations not affected. Failure to enforce any part of the Agreement does not affect validity of the Agreement. If the marriage is postponed, the Agreement will be enforceable; if the marriage is canceled, the Agreement shall be void. The entire

Agreement is in this writing and any changes must be made in writing. Georgia law governs, although the Agreement is binding even if you move to another state. Each of you has been represented by counsel of your choice.

16

PRENUPTIAL AGREEMENT

We, FIANCÉ, now a resident of _____ County, Georgia ("Fiancé"), and FIANCÉE, now a resident of _____ County, Georgia ("Fiancée"), for and in consideration of the premises and the mutual covenants and Agreements contained herein, and other valuable consideration, the receipt and sufficiency of which is hereby acknowledged, hereby agree as follows:

SECTION 1. PURPOSES AND GENERAL CONSIDERATIONS.

1.1 <u>Contemplation of Marriage.</u> We are contemplating marriage to each other in the near future, we intend to reside in _____ County, Georgia, and we wish to define our respective rights in our property and the property of each other, including rights each of us may acquire in the future. We agree that we are not married at this time.

1.2 <u>Disclosure and Disposition of Assets and Obligations.</u> We have fully considered our mutual rights and obligations, and are satisfied that each of us has made fair and reasonable disclosure and disposition of the nature, extent, and probable value of all our property rights and financial obligations.

1.3 <u>Acknowledgments</u>. We hereby acknowledge the following:

(a) We each acknowledge that there has been no pressure or influence on either of us from any third person and that this Agreement is voluntarily executed and entered into by each of us.

(b) Fiancé has correctly and accurately described to Fiancée the assets of his present personal estate. Fiancée acknowledges that her efforts have not contributed to the wealth or earning potential of Fiancé. Fiancé's financial statement, which he warrants is a comprehensive and complete listing of all of his assets and liabilities, is attached to this Agreement as Exhibit A and is incorporated herein by reference.

(c) Fiancée has correctly and accurately described to Fiancé the assets of her present personal estate. Fiancé acknowledges that his efforts have not contributed to the wealth or earning potential of Fiancée. Fiancée's financial statement, which she warrants is a comprehensive and complete listing of all of her assets and liabilities, is attached to this Agreement as Exhibit B and is incorporated herein by reference.

1.4 <u>Advisement of Rights.</u> We have each been advised of our rights in and to the other's estate under the laws of Georgia in the event of our marriage and a subsequent divorce or death of one of us without the execution of any prenuptial Agreement, including the rights of the survivor to an allowance for support from the other's estate, rights which could be conferred by the other's will, rights in the event of intestacy, and other transfers capable of renunciation or election. We have also advised each other as to any known probable increases in our present personal estates and as to the identity of our respective relatives and heirs-at-law and of our devisees and legatees under any existing will or will contemplated immediately after marriage. After consideration of all such information and advice, we have voluntarily negotiated and agreed upon the mutual promises and Agreements herein set forth

1.5 <u>Cooperation in Sale, Transfer or Designation.</u> If either one of us shall desire to mortgage, convey, sell, lease, or in any manner encumber or transfer any portion or any specific asset of either one's estate, real, personal, mixed, whether in whole or in part, or to designate a person other than our spouse as a beneficiary of a qualified plan, insurance policy or other plan or benefit, then each of us agrees that, on request of the other, we will execute any instrument of release, disclaimer, renunciation, quitclaim, discharge, waiver, conveyance, or otherwise which may be requested to further the purpose of this and all other provisions of this Agreement.

SECTION 2. CHARACTERIZATION OF PROPERTY.

2.1 <u>Separate Property</u>. The following described property shall be deemed for purposes of this Agreement to be separate property:

(a) All property that is owned by either of us before the date of our marriage, including without limitation cash, securities, employee benefits, tangible personal property, and real property, shall be the separate property of that party. Such separate property shall be solely controlled by that party and shall be subject to his or her disposition as his or her separate property in the same manner as though our marriage had not occurred.

(b) Without limiting the generality of this Agreement, each of us specifically agrees that Schedule A (attached hereto and made a part hereof) sets forth the separate property of Fiancé and that Exhibit B (attached hereto and made a part hereof) sets forth the separate property of Fiancée.

(c) All property either of us may hereafter acquire as the result of a gift, inheritance, bequest devise, or descent from a third party, together with the rents, income, profits, losses, and proceeds of sale or exchange thereof, whether acquired before or after marriage, shall be the separate property of the party who receives that property.

SECTION 3. PROVISIONS DURING MARRIAGE.

3.1 <u>Principal Residence</u>. Anything in this Agreement to the contrary notwithstanding, the following provisions shall govern the ownership and disposition of the real property we intend to own and occupy as our principal residence (the "Property") after our marriage:

(a) We shall hold title to the Property as tenants in common, with the respective percentages of ownership reflective of our initial monetary contributions to its purchase expense of $1.2 million. Any increase in the fair market value over $1.2 million, as determined by an average of three appraisals by MAI Appraisers, shall belong equally to Fiancé and Fiancée. This formula for determining ownership shall apply during marriage and in the event of divorce or death of either party.

(b) Fiancé shall be the sole obligor on any mortgage or other debt on the Property and he shall pay all other expenses (including, but not limited to, property taxes, insurance, repairs, and maintenance) associated with the Property.

(c) Fiancé shall pay all reasonable and necessary expenses to maintain our household.

(d) If we sell the Property during our marriage, we agree to divide the proceeds in accordance with the respective percentages of ownership.

3.2 <u>Operating Fund</u>. Fiancé shall provide Fiancée with a minimum monthly allowance of Three Thousand Dollars ($3,000.00); provided, however, that if Fiancé's gross annual income falls below Two Hundred Thousand Dollars ($200,000.00), then the monthly allowance contemplated by this section shall be reduced pro rata.

3.3 <u>Automobile</u>. Fiancé shall provide Fiancée with a new automobile every third year comparable to a Mercedes 500 Series vehicle and shall pay all associated expenses.

3.4 <u>Medical Expenses</u>. Fiancé shall provide Fiancée with medical insurance (group through his employment or private), if such insurance is obtainable, and he shall pay all of Fiancée's reasonable and necessary medical and dental expenses.

3.5 <u>Board Membership</u>: Fiancé shall appoint Fiancée to the Board of Directors of _____, Inc. and _____, Inc.

SECTION 4. PROVISIONS IN EVENT OF DIVORCE.

4.1 <u>Financial Settlement.</u> If we divorce, we agree as follows:

(a) If Fiancé initiates a divorce proceeding by filing a divorce complaint and having Fiancée served with a copy of the complaint, then Fiancé agrees that he shall give to Fiancée and Fiancée agrees that she will accept, in full settlement of all claims or rights she may otherwise have, an amount equal to the <u>greater</u> of a percentage of the net worth of Fiancé's separate property or a fixed dollar sum, determined as follows:

One (1) year of marriage	5 % or $500,000
Two (2) years of marriage	10% or $525,000
Three (3) years of marriage	15% or $550,000
Four (4) years of marriage	20% or $575,000
Five (5) years of marriage	25% or $600,000
Six (6) years of marriage	30% or, $625,000
Seven (7) years or more of marriage	33.33% or $650,000

Fiancé shall make any transfer under this section within thirty (30) days after the entry of a final decree of divorce. Any amounts due under this section may be paid in cash or in kind, but any payments made in kind shall be fairly representative of the overall appreciation or depreciation from its cost basis of Fiancé's separate property.

(b) If Fiancée initiates a divorce proceeding by filing a divorce complaint and having Fiancé served with a copy of the complaint, then Fiancé agrees that he shall give to Fiancée and Fiancée agrees that she will accept, in full settlement of all claims or rights she may otherwise have, an amount equal to the lesser of a percentage of the net worth of Fiancé's separate property or a fixed dollar sum, determined as follows:

One (1) year of marriage	5% or $100,000
Two (2) years of marriage	10% or $150,000
Three (3) years of marriage	15% or $200,000
Four (4) years of marriage	20% or $300,000
Five (5) years of marriage	25% or $350,000
Six (6) years of marriage	30% or $400,000
Seven (7) years or more of marriage	33.33% or $500,000

Fiancé shall make any transfer under this section within thirty (30) days after the entry of a final decree of divorce. Any amounts due under this section may be paid in cash or in kind, but any payments made in kind shall be fairly representative of the overall appreciation or depreciation from its cost basis in Fiancé's separate property.

4.2 <u>Marital Property</u>. Any other property acquired by us or either of us due to personal employment, services, time work, or efforts after the date of our marriage and while we are not living separate and apart shall be marital property and shall be owned in proportion to our respective contributions to such property. All rents, income, profits, losses, and proceeds of sale or exchange attributable to such property shall be allocated in the same proportions. In the event of our legal separation or divorce, we agree to exercise our best efforts to effect a division of such property, in cash or

in kind, including undivided interests in kind, or partly in cash and partly in kind, either pro rata or non pro rata, at a reasonable rate or rates of division value.

4.3 <u>Separate Property</u>. No separate property now or hereafter acquired shall be subject to or taken into account for purposes of making an equitable division or other property settlement.

4.4 <u>Principal Residence</u>. Fiancé shall have the right, exercisable upon written notice for up to sixty (60) days after the entry of a final order of divorce, to purchase Fiancée's interest in the Property for the fair market value of her respective percentage of ownership as set out in Section 3.1(a) of this Agreement, determined without consideration of any discounts for minority interest or lack of marketability. If Fiancé does not exercise his right to purchase Fiancée's interest in the Property, Fiancée shall have the same right, exercisable upon written notice for up to sixty (60) days after the expiration of Fiancé's right, to purchase Fiancé's interest in the Property. If neither of us exercises our right to purchase the Property from the other, then the Property shall be sold, and the proceeds shall be divided in accordance with the respective percentages of ownership.

SECTION 5. PROVISIONS IN EVENT OF DEATH

5.1 <u>Testamentary Provisions for Fiancée</u>. If Fiancé should predecease Fiancée, then in addition to and not in lieu of any other provisions Fiancé may make for Fiancée upon his death, Fiancé shall execute a Last Will and Testament or testamentary substitute, which shall include the following provisions:

(a) Fiancé shall name Fiancée a co-Executor with a financial institution of his choosing;

(b) Fiancée shall have the right to receive, either through testamentary provisions or otherwise, assets equal in value to one-third (1/3) of the value of Fiancé's estate as finally determined for Federal estate tax purposes;

(c) Fiancée shall have the option to include in her share all tangible personal property located in the principal residence;

(d) Fiancée shall have the option to include in her share Fiancé's portion of the principal residence. If Fiancée does not exercise this option, then she shall have the right to reside in the residence until it is sold.

5.2 <u>Testamentary Provisions for Fiancé</u>. If Fiancée should predecease Fiancé, then, in addition to and not in lieu of any other provisions Fiancée may make for Fiancé upon her death, Fiancée shall execute a Last Will and Testament or testamentary substitute, which shall include the following provisions:

(a) Fiancée shall name Fiancé a co-Executor with a financial institution of her choosing;

(b) Fiancé shall have the right to receive, either through testamentary provisions or otherwise, assets equal in value to one-third (1/3) of the value of Fiancée's estate as finally determined for Federal estate tax purposes;

(c) Fiancé shall have the option to include in his share all tangible personal property located in the principal residence;

(d) Fiancé shall have the option to include in his share Fiancée's portion of the principal residence. If Fiancé does not exercise this option, then he shall have the right to reside in the residence until it is sold.

SECTION 6.   CHANGES IN CHARACTERIZATION OF PROPERTY

6.1 <u>Property Shall Retain Its Character</u>. Except as otherwise specifically provided in this Agreement, any property owned by us or by either of us shall retain its character as separate property or marital property, as the case may be, through all its changes in forms notwithstanding any act or failure to act of either of us. Without limiting the generality of this Section 6:

(a) The character of property as separate shall not be altered, modified, or transmuted because of time, work, or efforts devoted to the investment, management, maintenance or improvement of such property by the other. Each of us acknowledges, understands and agrees that, but for this Agreement, one of us might have a claim on or right to some or all of the income, profits, appreciation, or assets derived from the time, work, or efforts of the other in the investment or management of the separate property of the other, and any such claim or right is hereby expressly waived.

(b) Each of us may devote all or part of his or her time, work, or efforts to the investment, management, maintenance, or improvement of his or her separate property, and such time, work, or efforts shall not create a marital property interest in such separate property. Each of us acknowledges, understands, and agrees that, but for this Agreement, one of us might have a claim on or right to some or all of the income, profits, appreciation, or assets derived from the time, work, or efforts of the other in the investment or management of his or her own separate property, and any such claim or right is hereby expressly waived.

(c) No amount of use or occupancy, permissive or otherwise, of the separate property of one of us by the other will in any way alter, modify or transmute the separate nature of such property except for the separate property of either of us that shall have been transferred by gift to the other evidenced in writing.

(d) The character of property as marital or separate shall not be altered, modified, or transmuted by any tax election or tax return or the filing of any other documents required by Federal, state or local governments.

(e) The use of any property to discharge any obligation of us or either of us shall not alter, modify, or transmute the character of any property not so used.

(f) The character of property as marital or separate shall not be altered, modified, or transmuted by the use of property of a character other than the character of such property to discharge any obligation related to such property.

6.2 <u>No Right to Reimbursement</u>. The debts contracted by either of us prior to our marriage are to be paid by the one who contracted the same without the property of the other being in any way liable for the payment thereof. If one of us expends all of his or her separate funds for family living expenses, or for the maintenance, insurance, and other costs directly attributable to the separate property of the other, he or she shall have no right thereafter to seek reimbursement for any such expenditures, unless otherwise expressly agreed between us in writing.

6.3 <u>Change of Character by Gift</u>. Either of us may transfer, convey, devise, or bequeath any property to the other either during the marriage or by Will. Neither of us intends by this Agreement to limit or restrict his or her right to receive any such transfer, conveyance, devise, or bequest from the other, and nothing in this Agreement should be construed as a waiver or renunciation by either of us of any such transfer, conveyance, devise, or bequest from the other.

SECTION 7.   GENERAL PROVISIONS.

7.1 <u>General Release</u>. Any and all claims, liens, demands, causes of action, obligations, damages and liabilities, known or unknown, that either of us has had in the past, or now has, or may have in the future against the other. Any and all other claims, liens, demands, causes of action, obligations, damages, and liabilities known or unknown, that either of us has had in the past, or now has against the other, including, without limitation, any claim based on any implied or express Agreement arising out of our co-habitation prior to marriage. Each of us expressly understands and acknowledges that it is possible that unknown losses or claims exist or that present losses may have been underestimated in amount or severity.

7.2 <u>Waiver of Rights</u>. Each of us hereby relinquishes, disclaims, releases, and forever gives up any and all rights, claims or interests in or to the property of the other, including but not limited to rights to an award of alimony or separate maintenance upon separation or divorce, claims of contribution to such property, rights as an heir or widow or widower, rights or claims of year's support, dower, or any statutory substitutes therefore as provided by the statutes of the jurisdiction in which one or the other or both of us might be domiciled, rights to any distributive share in property of the other who might die intestate, rights to take against the Will of the other, rights to a family allowance, rights to a probate or other homestead, and any right to act as administrator of the estate of the other.

7.3 <u>Support Obligations</u>. Nothing contained in this Agreement shall be construed as absolving us or either of us of statutory obligations of support during marriage, nor affect in any way the obligation to support any children of our marriage.

7.4 <u>Enforceability of This Agreement</u>.

(a) Failure of either Fiancé or Fiancée at any time to require the performance by the other party of any of the terms and conditions hereof shall in no way waive or otherwise affect such party's rights thereafter to enforce the same, nor shall the waiver by either party of any breach of any of the terms and conditions hereof be held or construed to be a waiver of any succeeding breach of such terms and conditions hereof or as a waiver of any term or condition itself.

(b) If marriage between us for any reason is deferred beyond the date now contemplated, this Agreement shall nevertheless subsist and be valid and enforceable according to its terms. If either of us declares that he or she will not marry the other or if our marriage does not occur or if either of us marries another person, this Agreement shall be null and void, and each of us then waives any and all rights and claims, other than any enforceable note or other obligation hereafter undertaken, against the other and his or her estate.

7.5 <u>Entire Agreement</u>. This Agreement constitutes our entire Agreement and supersedes and cancels any prior Agreements, representations, warranties, or communications, whether oral or written, between us regarding the transactions contemplated hereby and the subject matter hereof. Neither this Agreement nor any provision hereof may be changed, waived, discharged, or terminated orally, but only by an Agreement in writing signed by the party against whom the enforcement of such change, waiver, discharge, or termination is sought.

7.6 <u>Governing Law</u>. This Agreement shall be governed by and construed in accordance with the internal laws (and not the law of conflicts) of the State of Georgia.

7.7 <u>Counterparts</u>. This Agreement may be executed in two or more counterparts, each of which shall be deemed an original, but all of which together shall constitute one and the same instrument.

7.8 <u>Severability</u>. If any provision of this Agreement or application thereof to any person or circumstance shall be invalid or unenforceable to any extent, the remainder of this Agreement and the application of such provision to any other person or circumstance shall not be affected thereby and shall be enforced to the fullest extent permitted by law.

7.9 <u>This Agreement Binding</u>. This Agreement shall be binding and enforceable regardless of whether we become domiciled in another state (whether a "community property state" or "common law property state" or otherwise). This Agreement shall bind and be enforceable against the

parties hereto and their respective heirs, legal representatives, assigns, and successors in interest.

7.10 <u>Headings</u>. The section headings in this Agreement are inserted solely as a matter of convenience and for reference, and are not a substantive part of this Agreement.

7.11 <u>Representation</u>. Each of us has been advised that we are entitled to be represented in negotiations for and in preparation of this Agreement by independent legal counsel of our choosing, and each such counsel has explained the terms and implications of this Agreement. Each of us has read this Agreement and is fully and completely aware of its provisions and its legal effect.

IN WITNESS WHEREOF we have executed this Agreement on the _____ day of June, 2006.

Signed, sealed and delivered
In the presence of:

_____   _____
Witness   FIANCÉ

_____ (SEAL)
Notary Public

Date: _____

_____
Attorney for Fiancé

Signed, sealed and delivered
In the presence of:

_____   _____
Witness   FIANCÉE

_____ (SEAL)
Notary Public

Date: _____

_____
Attorney for Fiancée